Praise for Return to Love: Restoring the Heart of Christianity

"A few years back during a church retreat I was leading at Ghost Ranch in northern New Mexico, I had a casual conversation with a conference attendee. That attendee was Alena Van Dyke, and I must confess that after a few more conversations with her, I felt a bit like John the Baptist when Jesus came to be baptized. I felt Alena needed to be leading the conference so I could soak up her wisdom.

Alena has gained this wisdom through impartation and revelation from the Spirit as she's walked on bright mountaintops and through dark valleys. In these pages, she chronicles her journey and lessons learned through her experience of the vast love of God. You will be challenged, edified, and encouraged by reading, but beyond that, you will be enticed by the Spirit to know this love in ever-increasing measure for yourself."

Charlie Elmore
Pastor, Emmanuel Chapel, Albuquerque, NM

"*Return to Love* is practical, inspiring, and beautifully written. It offers an invitation into an exciting relationship with the Creator of the Universe. It is truly life-changing.

I felt as if I were sitting down with a friend as I read, and I didn't want to put it down. Alena shares her story in such a powerful and relatable way. She invites you to go deeper with God on a journey that is focused on relationship not religion. I smiled, cried and was encouraged as I read Return to Love and reflected on deepening my relationship with Christ. This book and the prayers within are both anointed and beautiful!"

Catherine Stuart
Author, *Potluck, A Sleepy Haven Mystery*

"Alena Van Dyke is a woman after God's own heart, who has wholeheartedly given herself over to Him and given us the way to go and do likewise! In her first book, *Return to Love*, she has put God first and given anyone who reads this a passionate plea to return to the lover of your heart and soul plus the tools that are necessary to enter into the most romantic love story of all time and into eternity. Sharing her heart, the ups and downs, ins and outs of living, Alena has been in and through the refiner's fire and has produced a treasure chest of pure gold for readers of all ages and times to take into their hearts and pour themselves out, as a drink offering before the creator of the universe, who so loved the world, that He gave us His Word. I know this book will be used by many to preach out of and teach into the hearts and minds of all who need to know these truths."

Bishop Mark Tross
Coordinator for NM Prayer Connect, Prayer At The Heart of NM and Church of God, NM & El Paso, TX

"You'll want to read this book no matter how long or short your walk with Christ has been. It's the invitation you've been waiting for to unlock the chambers of your heart that you thought were dead for good. It's safe to turn down this path you've been praying to appear. This is your moment to embark on the journey in and through, as you *Return to Love*. It's a yes. It's a now. It's a gift."

Jenna Sartor
Author, *Life's Golden Nuggets*

"This book gives you practical steps to grow in your relationship with the Lord. It will challenge you to take an introspective look at your heart, and bring newfound revelation of what it means to journey with the Lord and fall deeply in love with Jesus. While many Christian books are either all theology or all fluff, *Return to Love* balances the tendency to lean too far into legalism or cheap grace. It will show you how God loves and calls us in our mess, but never calls us to stay there. I've never read a book like this."

Dr. Paul Martinez
President, De Novo Concierge Pastors, Albuquerque, NM

Return to Love

Restoring the Heart of Christianity

Alena Van Dyke

Copyright © 2022 by Alena Van Dyke

All rights reserved. No part of this publication may be reproduced, stored or transmitted in any form or by any means, electronic, mechanical, photocopying, recording, scanning, or otherwise without written permission from the publisher. It is illegal to copy this book, post it to a website, or distribute it by any other means without permission.

Fair Use: No more than 100 words, consecutive or in total, may be refrenced or quoted without permission. This publication must be properly cited in a manner that conforms to a scholarly style. Ellipses (...) may not be used in ways that alter the ideas of the original work. Ministries may reproduce stand-alone quotations in bulletins or on documents to be shown on a screen provided that the source is fully documented and credited.

This is a work of creative nonfiction. Some parts have been fictionalized in varying degrees, for various purposes.

ISBN 979-8-9861601-0-8 (*paperback*)
ISBN 979-8-9861601-3-9 (*hardback*)
ISBN 979-8-9861601-1-5 (*ebook*)
ISBN 979-8-9861601-2-2 (*audiobook*)

Library of Congress Control Number: 2022909267

Unless otherwise indicated, all Scripture quotations are from The Holy Bible, English Standard Version® (ESV®), copyright © 2001, by Crossway, a publishing ministry of Good News Publishers. Used by permission. All rights reserved.

First Edition

Hearts by Daniel Cuenca
Photo by Emily Okamoto

Published by Miniphanies™ LLC
Albuquerque, New Mexico
www.miniphanies.com

*Dedicated to the one who restores our souls
& all who want to be restored.*

Psalms 23:3

Contents

Before We Begin...   1

0. Prologue   5
1. Return to Love   13
2. Desert Wanderings   27
3. Human Rollercoasters   51
4. Worthy of Love   73
5. Becoming Friends   101
6. Step-by-Step   123
7. Spiritual Family   141
8. The Invitation   161

Postscript
Continue on the Journey   181
About the Author   182
A little Love for my BFFs   184

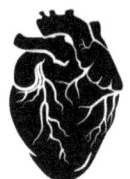

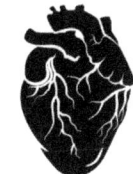

Before We Begin...

The Lord is like the ocean. He is wild and roaring, deep and unknown, and yet gentle, in the same way a wave comes to kiss your toes while you stand safely on the sand.

Many people often walk in the sand instead of in the waves. More often than not, many who think they're standing on a beach are really at a mirage in the desert.

I want to introduce you to an ocean of a God.
The ocean doesn't fit in a box.
Neither does the Source of all Creation.

I've spent some time like Jonah,[1] trying to hide or run away from this. I've spent some time like Peter,[2] denying my experience of him.
I've spent some time like Moses,[3] telling God he picked the wrong person and asking him to send someone else.

Sometimes I seem to think I know better than God.
Spoiler alert, I don't.

---
1 Jonah 1:3
2 Luke 22:54-62
3 Exodus 4:13

2 || Return to Love

All three of those men had intimate encounters with God at mighty waters. Jonah was thrown overboard and swallowed by a whale, Peter walked on water with Jesus, and Moses witnessed the sea part for Israel and then swallow the Egyptians. They got in the middle of the water and wrestled with themselves and with God's way. Every time, God met them.

I wrestle with God too.
He always meets me, and he always wins.
His win is my win.
When God wins, it means we get to do what we were created to do.

People in the Bible are named after their destiny, or what they brought into the world. My birth name literally means beautiful bearer of light, reborn, and one who lives by the dike or levee. A dam holds the water back, but a dike allows just the right amount of water through. A person on the dike walks along the water and repairs the breaches.[4]

I am called to stand on the bridge, or in the doorway, between God and his people.[5] I allow the Spirit of God to flow through me... to *you*.

Therefore, this book isn't just a book.
It's a doorway.

I'm inviting you to engage God in a new way. I'm inviting you to believe that a big, ineffable God loves you, likes you, pursues you, and is beckoning you to walk, play, laugh, dream, and wrestle with him through life.

Sometimes I say I'm in the reconciliation ministry, which is reconciling people to their true selves, each other, and the Divine. I tried to ignore this purpose, but every time someone said my name, it was there. In the book of Luke, Jesus says, "...if they keep quiet, the stones will cry out."[6]

There were seasons in life where it felt like even the stones cried out to me and told me I must speak.

---
4 Isaiah 58:12
5 Leviticus 8:33; Ephesians 2:11-22
6 Luke 19:40

I must write to you. I must tell you there is *more*. I am compelled.[7]

My life mission is to expand your God box.
That says so much, and yet, so little....

God's love is not out of reach. Knowing him is not just for pastors or teachers or priests. God loves you and wants you to know him.

No matter who you are, he's for you.
He wants you. Not just some of you, *all of you*.

Even when I hide, deny, or disagree with God, he still pursues me. He loves me, and I love him. This is what I've learned from standing in the waves. This is what I've learned as I've danced and wrestled with God.

I hope you choose to love and dance and wrestle with him too.
He *is* pursuing you, after all.

---

7 1 Corinthians 9:16

Prologue

I wrote this book for those who want to be spiritually Christian rather than religiously Christian.

Spirituality is personal and relationship-based. Spiritual living, therefore, is placing a transformative relationship with the living God at the forefront of every aspect of our existence. Rather than degrading our spiritual experience to impersonal religious practices, our world is crying out for a return to something more intentional. I believe the way to partake in a meaningful, limitless, satisfying life with God, is to shift away from following a set of rules and religion.

The commands God provided are good and even required, at some level, to live a fulfilling and happy life. Without structure, we would have chaos. But the structure man has built is not the same one God gave us. If we focus too much on the law, we will lose focus on love. If we keep looking at how life should look, instead of actually embracing the experience, the journey, and the relationship with God that's available to us, we will miss out. We will become more religious than spiritual. We will become more judgmental and accusatory and less introspective and humble.

Instead, we must make our axis the greatest commandment: loving the Lord with all of your heart, soul, and might and loving your neighbor as yourself. If we center our lives around Jesus, everything will rotate around his words. Christianity is the most fulfilling way[1] to live life.

Christian spirituality should be centered around how we are transformed from the inside out by our relationship with Jesus.

Life doesn't always fit inside the lines of the law and the neat religious box people would like it to fit within. That goes for both the pain and unexpected circumstances in life, as well as the mysteries of encountering God in an unexplainable, life-altering way. There is mystery and partnership available with God that you can only experience when you love and seek him like a friend. I'm here to remind the world that Jesus walks with us, even outside the lines. God walks with us in the darkness and pain as well as the light. He never leaves or forsakes us.[2] Even what is darkness to us, is light to him.[3]

I know there will be some readers who are feeling stuck and will not want their God box to expand. Change is hard for most people. People like organization and wish they could explain their lives within neat lines. But life doesn't work that way. Life is messy. This book might rock the boat, but if you're a Christian, you worship the God who commands the wind and waves to be still.[4] Have faith that he can and will calm any storm in your life.

If God led you to this book, he wants you to know more of him. He wants to show you he loves you and will be with you in any storm. There could be sections that are a little challenging to read. It's ok. You can do it. Put it down, take a breather, get a snack, and pray for God to tear down the lies so you can believe he really is good, more loving, and more holy than this book could ever express.

---

1 After Jesus ascended into heaven, those spreading the good news, called it "the way." See Acts 9:2; Acts 18:25-26; Acts 24:14.
2 Hebrews 13:5
3 Psalm 139:12
4 Mark 4:39-41

This Book is For...
This book is for those feeling spiritual disillusionment. I've been there. The season you're in won't last forever, friend. Let me renew your hope that not all Christians are the bad kind of crazy. Let me renew your faith that some people who believe in Jesus can be more open-minded than you ever thought, and still, be dedicated to the Word, the Spirit, and running after the heart of God. Balanced Christian spirituality requires that we stretch and expand by reconnecting with and loving our true selves, the Creator, and everyone he created.

This book is for those who don't just want to know *about* God, they want to *know* God. I've spent my life getting to know him and learning about him, from almost every tradition. There are tons of false gods people follow and worship: selfishness, money, sexuality, food, and more. The Bible introduces us to the King of Kings and Lord of Lords, the Creator of the universe. It shows us his heart and personality. Christianity is the only faith system that focuses on a personal relationship with the Father of the universe, his Spirit, and his Son. It is the only faith system that recognizes the limits and potential of our humanity and does not make equality with God something to be grasped. Instead, Christianity recognizes our need for a savior and claims that the savior was and is the Jewish man, Jesus of Nazareth. It claims God is the one who must bridge the gap between us and him, because we are incapable of perfecting ourselves. It is the only religion that reminds humanity, "God desires mercy, not sacrifice."[5] All your striving and sacrifices to be perfect, while sincere, are not actually what God wants. He wants your faith that Jesus is God and that truth will set you free. Christianity says call out to Jesus, in faith, and ask for him to enter your heart. Through this action, you will come to know him. Not through works or sacrifice, but through faith and love and surrender.

This book is for those who grew up in church and got hurt or jaded and left. It is especially for those who experienced a trauma like a church split, divorce, or abuse. God feels our pain, and he is fighting for you. While the church may have wounded you, the Healer wants to unite you with those who are still fighting alongside you for things to be better. God is not the

---
5 Hosea 6:6

church and the church is not God. I hope this will further your journey in differentiating God from the institution.

This book is for those who prayed to invite Jesus into their heart at some point in time but then didn't continue to seek him. If you never went any further to learn the Bible or who Jesus is, you might want to know why Jesus is such a big deal. And you probably want to learn about him in *common language*. I want you to feel like a friend of yours is introducing you to her BFF. Grab a cup of coffee, curl up in a comfy chair and let me chat with you about my story and my very good, faithful, generous, loving God.

This book is for those who live on the bridge between their church and "more;" meaning, they feel unsatisfied on Sundays and need a personal revelation from the Lord. You might have discovered that God is bigger than your church or community is willing to discuss. I want you to know you're not alone. God is with you. You might be at the beginning of an epic adventure. I want to encourage you, go on that adventure! The farther you go, the more it will all boil back down to the basics.

To get the most from this book, trust God is big enough to make space for all your questions and life experiences.

You might feel misunderstood or like a misfit, but God says, "*You belong, you are mine, and I love you.*" The God who is in control of the universe can handle your problems, fears, and anger. In fact, he wants to sort through all the questions with you. You might be surprised (or relieved) by how different his answers are from the scripted ones you've heard people preach.

God desires to do life *with* you.

There is *no reason* to hide or run from him.

The Creator of the universe, who introduced himself to Moses as the I AM, is more wonderful than the god Christians seem to reflect to the world. When God met Moses in the Old Testament, he introduced himself as "I AM who I AM"[6] or "I will be what I will be."

Don't you think that's a wild way for God to introduce himself?
He has no need to explain himself to us.
He will be what he will be.

In other words, *God is bigger than the box in which religion has tried to contain or explain him.*

As people minimize the power and presence and holiness of God, the impact of Christianity is proportionally reduced. This generation is not in awe of God. Our eyes worship the supernatural power of technology; not the God who turns water into wine, heals diseases, and raises people from the dead. Therefore, *the term "Christian" in our time and culture has been radically misused.* The perception of being Christian has changed from meaning "people who believe in Jesus, love God and others, and perform signs and wonders" to "people who hate ___, fill in the blank, all sorts of things." This is totally untrue, unbiblical, and simply false.

For years I didn't claim the descriptor, "Christian." I hated all it had come to stand for in the public view and knew if I used it, I would need a string of disclaimers. I've come to a place where I'm willing to use it and stand apart with my actions. I'm willing to try to redeem the true meaning of Christianity.

When Someone Claims to be Christian...
It should mean, "I love God with all my heart, mind, soul, and strength and love my neighbor as myself."[7]
It should mean, "I'm someone who believes Jesus Christ came and died on a cross and rose again to pave the way for everyone who believes to also become a new creation because he defeated sin and death."
It should mean, "I am a work in process, being transformed by how he loves me, forgives me, and walks through life with me."
It should mean, "I look forward to the coming kingdom and the lover of my

6 Exodus 3:14
7 Matthew 22:37-39

soul returning to set things right in the world, to bring justice and mercy, as only God can."

It should mean, "I believe Jesus is the way, the truth, and the life and the only way to abide in the love of the Father."[8]

It should mean, "I've asked the Holy Spirit to come live in me and guide me in everything, day by day, moment by moment."

It should mean, "I have made Jesus the Lord of my life and seek him wholeheartedly."

The book of John ends with him saying, "...there are also many other things that Jesus did. Were every one of them to be written, I suppose that the world itself could not contain the books that would be written."[9] Christian religion might have been boring to you, but meeting Jesus is exhilarating. There is so much more to be known.

This journey, this relationship, should be the most life-giving and most meaningful part of your life.

I seek to experience and know everything I can about God and what he has to say. I authentically, deeply, and sincerely, believe our life purpose is to be in intimate union with God. I do my best to seek God as a best friend and the lover of my soul who I can actually have a conversation with; as well as respect him as the King of Kings and the Uncreated Creator who is completely incomprehensible and more mysterious and wonderful than our brains could ever fathom.[10] The Hebrews calling God ineffable is the most accurate description.

The more we try to explain and name God, the more we limit him. At the same time, God *must* be named and explained to the best of our ability. Trying to describe God is like trying to describe falling in love. You can talk about your heart beating and the butterflies, but those are just symptoms. The mystery of attraction and chemistry and devotion is something that must be experienced. It is quite a task to try to put words to such a sacred subject.

---

8 John 14:6
9 John 21:25
10 John 15:14-15; Psalm 145:3; Isaiah 40:28; Ecclesiastes 3:11

I hope you will keep this in mind as you read this book. It can only express a *fraction* of God's beauty.

While I aim to live with God outside the box religion puts him in, he is always showing me my small perspective. This isn't something you do once. It's a life-long journey to see and know God, through vulnerability and relationship. Year after year, I stand upon the previous year's glass ceiling. I both honor and learn from my past, knowing I did the best I could with the knowledge I had at the time, and that this year, I will see and learn even more. I recommend that you do the same.

I'm not surprised by boxes and walls; we all have things that stand in the way of love. I am surprised by people's hunger. I wonder if this generation has been waiting for a book like this one. People tell me they have longed for someone to say these things out loud, and say them in a simple way, so they could understand. Simplicity is both powerful and fundamental to our nature.

Christianity must be reframed, redeemed, redefined.

The Christian way of life focuses on love, but most Christians today are not focused on loving God and each other so well that people will recognize us by our radical love. When asked, Jesus said, "'The most important [commandment] is, "Hear, O Israel: The Lord our God, the Lord is one. And you shall love the Lord your God with all your heart and with all your soul and with all your mind and with all your strength." The second is this: "You shall love your neighbor as yourself." There is no other commandment greater than these.'"[11] Later, he told his disciples, "A new commandment I give to you, that you love one another: just as I have loved you, you also are to love one another. By this all people will know that you are my disciples, if you have love for one another."[12]

God loved the world before it existed. He desires to be in loving communion with us, where his love overflows out of our hearts for him and for the <u>world around us.</u> We will explore this mysterious love story between us and

11 Mark 12:29-31
12 John 13:34-35

our Creator because learning to love and being known and loved in return, will transform you.

This is the heart cry of Jesus: "I love you and desire you so much, I came to earth to die for you. I destroyed the wall between the physical and spiritual realm, between the common and the holy,[13] so you could draw near to me and abide in my love. I want to know you and be known by you. I want you to receive my love and love me with all your heart, mind, and strength."

What kind of God says this!?
What kind of God gives up his own life for yours?
What other god has ever made himself the servant-leader of humanity, showing us how to love and serve others by his example?

Only this one, the one true God, Jesus Christ, who shows us what true love really looks like.

Let's redeem Christianity with that kind of love...
wholehearted, vulnerable, abiding, consistent, mysterious,
transformative love....

Let's return to love.

---

[13] Matthew 27:51

Return to Love

Before you were born, the Creator of the universe was singing over you. He wrote a plan and a purpose for your life. He had big dreams for you. He knit you together and made you with a desire for love. He put his very breath in you, so that you would be dependent on his continued gift of breath to live. The God of all things brought you into an epic adventure, a love story between his holy and humble son and a bride who resists his love and his ways until she loves him in return.

In this love story, you are the bride. Jesus knows every detail of your life, and still loves you more than you could ever fathom. He sits in heaven, and constantly asks the Creator for all of your heart every day and every moment of your life. He desires and longs and waits patiently and kindly to hear a weak, "yes," on your lips, so he can lavish his unquenchable love upon you.

Long before you were born, he died in the most humiliating way so he could ask for you. So that you might say, "Yes." The most humble, gentle, happy, and kind man who ever lived was killed by an angry mob because his love was so counter-cultural.[1] He embodied and represented the heart of the Father, the love of the Creator. The religious leaders of the day who

---
1 And he let them.

enforced the law, chose the law over love. They chose rules and religion over the openness of the Father's heart.

The law is how we define right from wrong. When we have legal rules and boundaries, it's easy to see where we fail or succeed. We can measure it easily: in or out, black or white. It's not so in love. Love is messy. It's emotional. When in love, we give above and beyond normal boundaries. In love, we put others first.

Our views of love and marriage have been so distorted in our culture that we can barely grasp the meaning of love. For many, love led to divorce or abuse. It led to a selfish partner who was only in the relationship for their own gain. It led to learning we were not enough. The culture of our world defines love as what we can get from someone.

It's time to return to the Bible's definition of love.

If I say, "God loves you," but you don't really know what true love is, you may hear that God wants to take advantage of, abuse, or use you for his own purposes. Nothing could be further from the truth. God sent his own flesh and blood to pave the way for us to be able to return to love. All love comes from him.[2] In order to love him, love ourselves, and love others, we need his indwelling Spirit to have its way in our heart. He is the only one who can heal our wounds, give us peace, and clean out all that hinders love. His loving-kindness brings us to a place where we can turn away from all our other lovers and all the comforts we think will fill or numb the love shaped hole in our hearts.

God's love is patient and kind. It does not envy, it does not boast, it is not arrogant or rude or proud. Love does not dishonor us or insist on its own way. It is not self-seeking or selfish. God's love is not easily angered, it is not irritable or resentful. God's love keeps no record of wrongs. Love does not delight in evil but rejoices with the truth. Love always protects, always trusts, always hopes, always perseveres. It bears all, believes all, and endures <u>all things. Love ne</u>ver ends and never fails.[3]

2 1 John 4:7
3 1 Corinthians 13:4-8; with adjustments from the author.

Only this kind of love will truly satisfy the longing deep in our souls.

As someone who comes from a divorced family, and one who is divorced myself, twice, I understand the resistance to love. For those of us who have personally felt and experienced the brokenness of what we thought was love, we hear, "love never ends," and sarcastically think "***yeah right***."

In June 2019, only weeks after my divorce was final, I heard God say, "I want you to get married again."

I cursed,
while I paced back and forth in a prayer room.

"Heck no.[4]
No way.
I'm not interested and I don't want to talk about it."

After my divorce, I planned to be some strange hybrid of a non-denominational-Christian-mystic-nun for the rest of my life. When the Lord spoke and shined a light on my resistance to marriage, I was instantly able to recognize the state of my heart. I was deeply convicted. I didn't know my determination to be single came from woundedness and the hardness of my heart until it was pointed out.

Within seconds of my eyes being opened, I made a spiritual u-turn. I prayed, "I'm sorry, Lord. I didn't know that was in there. Your will be done, not mine. If you want me to get married again, I trust you have a plan and a person, and you know what you're doing. If I'm here because you want to heal and soften my heart over the next six months and prepare me for marriage again, I'll do it. Do whatever is needed."

I felt peace, and then....
"He's the one," said the Lord, when I happened to turn and see a man standing near the back wall.
"That's not funny, Lord."

---

[4] I definitely said something worse than heck, but I'm keeping it PG for you.

I wanted to faint.
Shock took over.
"You have got to be kidding."

Silence.

I just kept pacing; getting closer, walking away, getting closer, walking away...and then wondered, "Is this real?" He was kneeling in the back, praying. I feared I was going crazy. I knew I was hearing the voice of God—that wasn't unusual to me. But could he really mean what I thought he meant? I hadn't talked to the man. I only knew his name. We had interacted once or twice. I'd seen him from afar. I didn't know all the suffering he'd gone through. I didn't think he could love me. Honestly, I didn't even know if I could love again.

When people hear about Jesus, it feels just like that. It's as if God is saying, "I know a man who is head over heels for you, and he wants to walk through life with you."

Our hearts resist that kind of commitment and love. Even if we already know someone, we resist the next level of love. Our heart replies, "No way, not interested. That's too good to be true. It can't be real. People have hurt me. I don't trust anyone to actually love me, to stay no matter what, to stick with me through thick and thin...if he knew me and my background, he wouldn't want me."

But God's Spirit won't back down. "No really, Jesus is the One. The One and only. He wants you. He's the lover of your soul and he knows everything about you. He's kneeling before his Father, asking for your heart, asking if he can be with you forever."

It's true.

I was brought up in a Christian home, so when I was a little girl, Jesus got a "Yes, I believe in you" from me. That tiny "yes" turned into a relationship, and I got to know God as Father, Son, and Holy Spirit. In my early thirties, my life seemingly fell apart. I walked through a Job season,[5] losing my husband, friends and family, closing my businesses, and moving across the country. God invited me into a new life, which began with an internship at a prayer room in Kansas City. I planned to rest and realign myself to the life God wanted for me. I planned to heal and pray and do my best to surrender and act on whatever he told me to do. I had built my life the best I knew how, and everything had crumbled and burned to the ground. I wanted to see if it was actually possible to love God with my whole heart, mind, and strength as we're commanded to do; and if what the Bible said was really true... if I focused solely on him, would he really, actually, take care of everything else?[6]

What if I lived off savings and dedicated myself full-time to pursuing Jesus?
Could I know what it felt like to be Mary of Bethany, washing Jesus' feet with her hair?[7]
What would happen to my soul and my relationship with God if I took all my worldly dignity and a year's worth of wages, and poured them out at the feet of Jesus like she did?

Isn't that what the Bible tells us to do?
To give him our all?

What if I traded my reputation and social prominence to go where no one knew me and pray in a grey chair under fluorescent lights in the Midwest? All through the night?
What could possibly come out of basically sitting and dedicating over eight hundred hours in six months to prayer?

I wish I had language at the beginning to express the deep longing in my soul to draw close to the Creator of the universe. When my world fell apart, I had nothing to rely on except the Lord, and he was all I wanted. Some might say that's a crutch, but it's really not. God is no more or less something you

---

5   Job is a book in the Bible about a man who loses everything: his family, wealth, health, everything; and is humbled and then restored by God. We'll talk about him again soon.
6   Luke 12:31
7   Matthew 26:6-13; Mark 14:3-9; Luke 7:36-50; John 12:1-8

rely on than your best friend or your spouse. When your world is falling apart, you call your best friends, and they walk through life with you.

On a more practical level, it only makes sense to seek the source of all wisdom when your world falls apart. Even the advice of your best friends can be fueled with anger and bias. When we need the truth, which is all the time, in good and bad seasons, God is the only place to turn. You could try to search for answers in the bottom of a bottle. You could try to escape your problems by sleeping around. You can avoid healing by pointing fingers at all the things that hurt you, including the church. But the only one with all the answers, who will sit in the pile of crap with you and help sort through it all, is Jesus. He is the one who loves you more than you love yourself, who died for your beautiful and messy life.

Within a year, my heart was going to be completely different; and all I had to do was sit in one of those uncomfortable grey chairs. Which, by the way, is the understatement of the century. I didn't just sit in a prayer room; I spent hours sorting through all the pain of life and making peace with painful memories from my past. I spent hours asking him to help me cleanse away anything that stood in the way, any barrier to fully knowing his love for me, and being able to live out the great commandment: loving God with all my heart, mind, and strength.[8] I prayed for friends and family and watched their lives change. I praised him in the midst of the emotional storms, and decided to believe God is good, even when my life was not.

Spending eight hundred hours in the presence of the Lord is not for the faint of heart. I used to think self-help books and personality tests made me introspective. That's *nothing*.

The inner healing that comes from actually engaging with the Holy Spirit for hours on end is unmeasurable.

You don't have to be at a house of prayer to engage with the Lord. God is everywhere. Anywhere you are able to listen, he will speak. Still, it's pretty wonderful to have a live band pray and worship with you all night long.

---

[8] Mark 12:30-31

I'm very glad those transformative hours occurred while sitting in a room full of musicians and intercessors in a very cold and humid place called Kansas City.

When God told me to move to Kansas City, I didn't know why. I was walking out of this Job season and sitting at church when a woman called me out of the congregation to give me a word from the Lord. She said God was giving me a spiritual pearl necklace for all the pain I'd been through and that it was time to paint a new life. Shortly after, I figured out what painting a new life meant. I got clear directions, to go to Kansas City for an internship at a night and day prayer room, and join the Nightwatch. When the Lord gives us the next step, we often don't know the result or why it's the next step. We're simply invited a little further into the love story he has written for us.

We all know love is best expressed in story form. Falling in love is better explained in feelings and experiences than data on a spreadsheet. The same goes for the Lord. Someone can tell you the man they love is 6'7" and has dark hair, but the data won't tell you about his character, integrity, sense of humor, and how he protects and cares for their heart. If I want to introduce you to Jesus, the man I love, you need to know our love story.

Some friends you speak to every month or so. Others, every week. Your best friend, a kindred spirit, a housemate, you might talk to almost every day. Then, there is one friend you do life with. You fall in love and decide to grow old with your spouse. You build a life together, you raise a family together, you make decisions together. Every night that person is there when you fall asleep and every morning when you wake.

Jesus wants to be that kind of best friend with you. He doesn't want an hour a day, whenever you're alone, driving, reading, drinking coffee in the morning, or reviewing your day as you fall asleep. He wants to be the one you talk to all day long. He wants to be there for you, and have your back, no matter what life brings. But he also understands every friend starts as an acquaintance. He doesn't expect you to be able to trust him with all your heart day one. The choice is instant, but living it out is a process.

Even though I had known Jesus since I was a little girl, I hadn't "honeymooned" with him. I hadn't spent a season pouring out my love upon him, giving him all my time and attention, and getting to know him. For many of us who grew up in Christianity, we were told our whole lives who God was and what we needed to do or not do to please him. That isn't first-hand experience; it is word of mouth rumors about a celebrity you haven't met. I did have a relationship with Jesus, thank God, but I still had a lot of beliefs that I absorbed through others.

Jesus was sincerely invited into my life, but I didn't always work my daily life around him. It was like we were dating, but not married yet. I went to church. I did a lot with him. I was writing about him and teaching about him, which required talking to him as much as possible. I went on vacations and spiritual retreats with him. I had spent my life getting to know him, even with formal education. I studied him and what the Bible said and what the world said.

But did I *love* him? I couldn't answer that question confidently. I said he was my all, but really, he was just one of my best friends. I wanted to love him, but I didn't know how to be all in, with all my heart, mind, and soul, like he commanded.

The one we love is worth all our time and attention, simply because we love them.

When you let yourself be fully known, and get to know someone fully (not that we can ever fully know or fathom this uncreated, ineffable God), it requires vulnerability. It requires time and trust. It requires love and faith. In rending our hearts, we walk through the fire of testing, through transformation, through tearing down everything that stands in the way of loving Him.

This is the hardest and most exhilarating and most important thing you'll ever do. What starts with weak faith becomes more real than reality. The more I saw God work around me, watching prayers manifest physically, right before my eyes, the more I wanted to know him. I asked, "Who are you? How could you be this good?"

This generation avoids marriage because we're avoiding broken promises. If we don't get married and the relationship ends, it's exactly what we expected and we're not as disappointed. If we commit to the vows of marriage and it fails, it triggers all the pain from our childhood, all the pain from our previous breakup or our parent's or grandparent's divorces. To love fully is to go all in and be vulnerable, and we avoid it. Avoiding the vulnerability feels safer. We can keep our hearts behind a few walls of protection by avoiding marriage. But without jumping in with both feet, we always have one foot outside the door. The end of the relationship is inevitable.

Couples who have stood the test of time together dove in with both feet. They went deeper when things got tough. They held each other closer when the world or storms of life tried to pull them apart. When life was hard, they found a tender-hearted lover to come home to; they had a safe place to run. When conflicts arose, they chose vulnerable connection instead of fight, flight, or freeze.

Jesus is the safest lover.

He loves your smile, the way you walk, your laugh. He holds you close when you cry. He delights in you. He knows every detail about you and longs to comfort and heal every internal and external wound.[9] He will never leave you or forsake you.[10] He went to defeat hell so you don't have to. He is patient when you're cranky. He will woo you back to him when you're angry. He will always pursue you and he will never stop, no matter how many times you reject him, spit in his face, refuse him, or deny him.

He loves you.
He's truly patient and kind.
He's deeply humble and generous.
He's sincerely for you in every way, and he will never leave.

9 Luke 12:7
10 Deuteronomy 31:6

Jesus wants to make a great exchange with us. He wants to take the things we have burned to the ground and give us a beautiful life. He wants to take our sorrow and heavy hearts and give us joy, hope, and gratitude. He never asks for anything without offering something better in exchange. He will ask us to give up the things that hold us back, and stretch ourselves into uncomfortable vulnerability and love for others, but it's always worth the love he offers.

The whole reason we're living, the reason we wake up in the morning with breath in our lungs, is to love him with all we have.

We're here to learn to love, and it's not easy. To love God and others and ourselves is hard at first. It's hard because we have to throw away everything culture taught us and follow Jesus instead of the instructions we were given by the world, the church, or our imperfect parents.

We are told success is being on top. Survival of the fittest is a climb to the top in our world. We're taught the more things and money we have, the more pride we have in our work, the more gossip we know, the more independent we are, the better we are. We're told the higher up in the corporate ladder we can get, the better, safer, more secure we will be. We don't learn it's a lie till we get hit elsewhere: with cancer, death, divorce, famine, or illness. When we get hit with something outside of our control, we realize it's not our business or busy-ness that brings us any safety. All the things we control, all the things within our power, can't help us get our health back, our spouse back, or our old life back.

Choosing Jesus' way, the way of love, means we have to redefine our lives. We must redefine success, redefine what's good, redefine love. We have to see ourselves, the world, and God differently. So many of us toil all the days of our lives, and it's meaningless.[11] We choose to fight or avoid pain, and give all of our attention to the storms of life. We choose to work ourselves to death for the valuable material things here on Earth instead of the thing that really matters: giving and receiving love with God and with each other.

---

11 Ecclesiastes 1:2

Until you taste it, you can't understand the value of that love. Jesus told a parable to explain it. He said a businessman, who specialized in jewelry and pearls, found a pearl of great value and buried it in a field. Then he took all he had in the world and sold it to buy the field.[12]

High quality pearls are made through an oyster's irritation and suffering over the course of many years. Most people think it's a piece of sand in an oyster that creates a pearl, but it's often a parasite. Whether caused by earth or bug, great value comes from great suffering. Shame, sorrow, hatred, betrayal, anxiety, depression, and mental illness...these kinds of things are parasites. Miscarriages, divorce, losing a loved one, illness, and other major stressful events are parasites that can create spiritual pearls.

There are beautiful people and bitter or dejected people.
The latter let the parasite eat their heart.
Beautiful people partner with God to turn the parasites into pearls.

Choosing to love Jesus more than anything else means taking all we have and trading all the little pearls for the one pearl of great price. The jewelry expert knows everything he owns is worth nothing compared to the value of this one thing. And that one thing is defined by David in Psalm 27:4. "One thing have I asked of the LORD, that will I seek after: that I may dwell in the house of the LORD all the days of my life, to gaze upon the beauty of the LORD and to inquire in his temple."

If we cling to Jesus, no matter our circumstances, then we can embody a life of love. When we know a good God stands with us and loves us as he seemingly gives and takes away[13] all the tiny, annoying parasites, we will trust him and let him shape the great pearl of our life.

*To seek the Lord is the **one thing** that matters.*

It's the only valuable thing we can do in this life: seek his love, dwell with him, wonder at his beauty and goodness, inquire of him with others.

---

12 Matthew 13:45-46
13 Job 1:21

I love the Lord for who he is.
He is unchanging.[14]
He is jealous for us.[15]
He loved us before we could love him.[16]
He desires our love.
He desires that we love him with all our heart, mind, and strength.[17]

When you love someone, you want to be with them. You want to share secrets with them. This requires drawing close and listening to them. In order to spend time with a new love, we have to make time and space for him or her in our lives.

In order to return to love, we have to make space for it. In my internship, praying through the night meant sleeping through the day. On top of a rigorous schedule, the internship required me to deny myself from many other types of distractions: movies and TV, parties, new romantic relationships, etc. I was invited to set aside my time and dedicate my undivided attention to my relationship with God.

Just to be clear, I'm not promoting any places or programs. The path I took may not be the best way for you to connect with God. He will take you on your own custom path. I won't even suggest that the places I went are the best way to connect with God. I might even say the opposite today. At the time, it was the right place for me to grow. For others, myself included, the peaceful quiet of my house during the COVID-19 lockdowns was just as transformative, maybe more so.

You don't have to be somewhere special to dedicate a season to journey through the depths of your heart with Jesus. The internship didn't change me. God did. The environment was just a tool God used to unlock something in my heart and life. Bible study, community, prayer, and fasting were highways to inner healing.

---

14 Psalm 102:27; Hebrews 13:8
15 Deuteronomy 4:24; 2 Corinthians 2:11
16 1 John 4:19
17 Deuteronomy 6:5

When you sit with your Creator for six consecutive hours, six nights a week, you learn how to *just be* with the one you love. You start to grasp and accept that you're loved, just as you are. You learn you're enough. You enjoy beholding and blessing the one who loved you first.

You learn to receive his love in return.

He's inviting you to see how much he loves you.
All you have to do is ask.

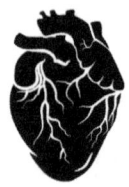

Invitation to Prayer

Lord, Do you really love me?
Is it true that you died for me and rose again? Is it true that you're up there in heaven, praying for me every moment, asking for me to love you, and contending for me to live the best life you dreamed for me?
Show me.
Open my eyes to see from your perspective. Open my ears to hear your loving voice. Let me know you. Search my heart and know me, so I can find you and know your heart. This world is full of darkness and pain and many voices that tell me what they think is best. Everyone has picked a side and everyone has an opinion.
I want your opinion, Jesus. I want your voice to be louder than any other.
I want your humble leadership and your wholehearted love to guide my heart. I want your indwelling Spirit to transform me.
I want to know your love, a love that is patient, kind, unselfish and forgiving. I want to experience a love that always protects, always trusts, always hopes, always dignifies me.
I want to know and feel your love, which never ends.
Reveal yourself to me. Reveal to me the truth of your love. Show me how much you love me and teach me how to love you in return.
Let it be, Amen.

Desert Wanderings

We were born into a cosmic love story, where the Son of God is asking to save his bride from her captor. It's the most classic love story we're told time and again. In many fairy tales and novels, a princess is captured by an evil witch, creature, or aspiring world-ruler. The prince who loves her somehow knows exactly where she is and what to do to rescue her. Sometimes, the princess must cry out for her prince to come rescue her. In real life, Jesus knows exactly where we are and how to rescue us, but it takes time before we cry out and want to be rescued. Often, our personal prison has great food, fun company, and promises to share in the evil plan for world domination.

If we think we're alone in this predicament, it's important to remember that even Jesus was led into a desert to be tempted to turn away from the Lord. This mystery is profound, that Jesus, who was fully God and fully man, fasted for forty days to be brought to his weakest point. He was driven by the Spirit of God to a place where he could be tempted with instant gratification. He was challenged with three things.[1]

First, the tempter asked him to use his own power to prove himself and make bread for himself. Jesus refused and basically said, "What God says

---
[1] Matthew 4

about me, his word, is more important than what you think. It's more important and has more value in my life than proving myself to you. I don't have to prove myself. I trust God to provide for me, I don't need to act in my own strength and power to change my circumstances. He is good, and if I'm hungry right now, there is a reason."

Second, the tempter took him to a high place and told him to jump off the ledge. He quoted the Bible at Jesus, implying, "God promises to protect you and send angels to keep you safe, so let's see if it's true, Jesus. Let's see if he actually loves you and will rescue you from a bad situation. If he loves you, he'll prevent you from even stubbing your toe, right? Jump!"

Jesus knew the scriptures too, and quoted the Word right back at him. "It is also written: 'Do not put the Lord your God to the test.'"[2] Jesus knows to test the Lord is to mock him. There is a big difference between falling on accident and jumping off a cliff. While both are tragic, one situation is the world happening to us, and the other is our free will choosing death over life. The Lord gives us free will, and Jesus would not test the Lord on this. He trusted God's perfect will over his own.

Last, the tempter takes Jesus to an even higher place and shows him all the kingdoms of the world. He shows them all their splendor, how beautiful and fruitful the land is, the hurting people he could rescue, and all the wealth in the land that he could use to set things right. He tugs on his heart strings. Jesus would have wanted to make the world better. He would have desired to set things right. The tempter says "I will give you all of this, all the power you want to do whatever you want with the whole world, if only you will worship me."

Jesus replies, "Get away from me! Tempt me no more! I will no longer listen to your lies or charades. I will not serve your kingdom or worship you! I will do what is right, I will obey what the Lord has commanded, to 'Worship the Lord your God, and serve him only.'[3]

---

2 Matthew 4:7
3 Matthew 4:10

I know in time, the whole world will be mine. I trust the Father's promise to me. I know in the right timing, his timing, everything you're showing me will be restored to its rightful kingship. I will not take it before it is given to me. I trust my Father's will and timing over my own."

Jesus made a free will choice to serve God. He chose to defer his desires to the Father even when tempted with proving himself, using his own power, or doubting God's goodness. He had decided to not take what he wanted before it was freely given to him. Jesus chose God's way over his way, even to death on a cross.

Jesus plays the long game.
Jesus is still asking and waiting on the Father.
He's still asking for the promises he's been given to manifest in the Earth.[4]

He's asking for *you*.

He will not take you or rescue you from the culture and lies of this age, until you give yourself freely to him. Jesus knows we won't appreciate his loving arms until we're ready. He is patient and kind while we search the world for pleasure and identity outside of him. He lets us wander. He knows exactly what we need to experience to appreciate him. He knows who needs a gentle breeze to cry out for help, and who needs a hurricane. If he comes to our rescue before we're ready, we will treat him like an admirer who brings us nice gifts, but not someone we appreciate or respect. We'll take the gift and send him away without changing our behavior. Until we turn our hearts towards him, we're not ready.

Love that's forced isn't love.

Jesus wants to woo us in the midst of our life circumstances. He wants to reveal his character over time. He reveals himself at a speed we can handle. He will prove himself faithful to stand by us and direct our path even when we're falling for his counterfeit. Turning our heart fully towards him takes time.

---

4 Psalm 2

Return to Love

When I was little, I accepted Jesus into my heart. I was raised in a Christian home. Reflecting on my childhood, I remember most that my parents desired to follow Jesus. Life wasn't about religion, it was about having a relationship with Jesus and living life his way: loving God and loving others. I distinctly remember a conversation where they told my brother and I that they picked our church because it was the closest thing they could find to a place that taught their beliefs.

That simple truth was a powerful force in my spiritual formation. Hearing this place was "the closest thing they could find," meant:

1. The church could be wrong.
2. My parents could be wrong.
3. Everyone was just trying to figure it out; which meant we could all change our minds over time and;
4. I was allowed to ask questions. I could seek and find[5] my own understanding of God's truth as I read his Word and got to know Jesus one-on-one.

My parents had no idea what they were doing at that moment, and I'm so glad. I firmly believe God was very pleased[6] with this initial setup. I really believe he created this ideal situation to make me who I am.[7] It couldn't have happened any other way.

I attended a Lutheran elementary school, and a charismatic Vineyard-type church that was technically Assemblies of God. On the weekdays, I was taught by grace alone we're saved by faith in Jesus, and we get to know him through the Bible. I was taught tradition and liturgy. On the weekends, I was taught we can all have a personal experience and relationship with God through listening to his voice and we can manifest special gifts he gives every one of us. I was taught it was normal for him to speak and move miraculously in individual lives.

Many Christians receive teachings in the Spirit or the Bible. From a very young age, I got both. I was getting the best of both worlds and the worst

---

5 Matthew 7:7-8
6 See Genesis 1. God is repeatedly pleased with his Creation.
7 Proverbs 20:24; Psalm 37:23; Jeremiah 1:5; Ephesians 1:11

of both worlds. While I had twice as much knowledge and experience to confirm my faith, I had twice as much religious baggage.

In middle school, I encountered the Lord in a life-altering experience. After this, I knew without a doubt I was going to dedicate my life to God by going into ministry of some kind. When I was graduating high school, I told my parents I wanted to go into a ministry training program and my Dad told me I couldn't go. I sobbed and yelled. I begged him to pray about it before he put his foot down. I knew in my core that I was supposed to be "in ministry." At eighteen, I knew in every blood cell, in every bone, in every breath. I knew I had to tell the world how much God loved them. Dad said, "No."

I felt like my destiny was derailed. I will never forget my Dad saying even if he must be accountable to God for stopping me, I was going to the University of New Mexico (UNM) whether I liked it or not. I struggled for nine years with a belief that my Dad didn't want me to go into ministry or thought I couldn't preach because I was a woman. He never said that. The truth was that I had a scholarship to UNM and my debt-free college experience was of the highest importance to my parents.[8]

They weren't worried about me missing my calling. They understood the value of a free undergraduate degree, and they wouldn't let me throw away such a huge blessing. I was eighteen and didn't have eyes to see. They had the life experience to know if God wanted me to do something, he would make it happen no matter where I studied.

My *plan*
was harshly altered
by God's *process*.

For a kid who was preaching in middle school, I was all of a sudden challenged by the idea that this wasn't my life path. I was lost and unsure why I felt this call to "more" while family and circumstances seemed to hold me back. I didn't understand life was a journey that required surrendering

---
[8] This is my chance to publicly thank my Dad for my debt-free undergraduate degree and apologize for whatever I said while I sobbed and yelled. Thank you, Dad.

to the timing of the Lord. I thought I had to chase his direction and obey and make it happen myself. I was clueless.

While I floundered and my heart yelled, "What am I doing here!?" God was quiet. He had a one-of-a-kind training program in mind, and I couldn't see it yet. After wandering through prerequisites, I realized there was a religious studies program available at UNM. I don't know how I missed it before that moment. I had been blinded by a foggy, angry, emotional storm, and I couldn't see the opportunity available.

I could not justify spending my time studying anything other than God. I didn't care if it was what the rest of the world thought about God. I was determined to get as close as I could to learning about him. That moment didn't feel like a God moment when it happened. I probably smacked myself on the forehead and asked myself, "Why didn't you think of that sooner?" That moment of revelation is still so clear to me, I know it was a moment of divine intervention. I know exactly where I was walking, between the duck pond and Mitchell Hall on the UNM main campus.

When it's God, it sticks with you. You can't forget.

Fast forward. Five years after graduating with my BA in Religious Studies, I was laying on an acupuncture table and I heard God say, "You will apply to George Fox and you will start in August."

If you haven't heard God's voice, I want you to know, it's often like a whisper and a knowing more than something that's almost audible. But sometimes he's direct. That day, God was direct and clear and loud. I probably should have trembled at his fatherly command, but I laughed. I laughed like Sarai laughed in the Old Testament when she was ninety and God said she would have a baby.[9] I laughed like God was an idiot. I laughed like he had no idea what he was saying.

If you need proof God doesn't strike you down in wrath, there you go. He could have repaid my laughter with lightning, and with those needles

---
9 Genesis 18:12

in me, I would have been bacon on the table. But just like the patient and loving God of Abraham, he has loving-kindness for me. I heard again, with a firm but gentle voice, "You will apply to George Fox and you will start in August."

God likes to repeat himself.

When you hear him say something multiple times,
you know it's him, and he means it.

You can't miss the path he wants you to go on. If you pass it by, he'll bring it up again and again. Over time, I've tried to learn to obey sooner, but I'm human. The first-time God says, "Go," I ask questions. But the second or third or fifth time, I finally learn to take him seriously and get moving.

When God spoke, I knew he meant an Evangelical Seminary in Oregon. Previously I had considered attending but their Spiritual Formation program was only for local students. At that time, I couldn't pick up my life and move to Portland. I went straight home from acupuncture and I looked up the program again. They were offering it as an online hybrid for distance learning students. I was floored. I thought that path was forever closed.

I contacted them and talked to the same lady in the admissions office I had years before. She informed me it was past the deadline to apply, but if I could submit my application by the next week, she could push it through because there was grace through the holiday. She said "I knew years ago you were supposed to come here. Your name is still on my desk. I've been praying for you all this time." I was stunned. Within ten days of laying on the acupuncture table, I had sent my application including the three letters of recommendation I needed. God conspired to work it all together within the deadline.

I had just taken the jump to quit my day job and risk being self-employed. To the world, this seemed like the most irrational timing to go back to school, but when the program required traveling six to eight weeks per year, I knew the Lord had created a divine setup for me. What job would have given me that much time off and been flexible for my graduate-level homework? I saw it as a confirmation that the two coincided. God knew what he was doing.

At the time, I told people I felt like I was building Noah's ark.[10] If you don't recall, Noah's story is how God tells him something that has *never* happened before is going to happen and he needs to dedicate almost ten percent of his life preparing for it. Noah is told by God that it's going to rain and gives him instructions to build an ark, a large boat that will house his family and every kind of animal that lives on land or in the air while the world is flooded. Noah has inspirational faith; he actually believes God and obeys him. On the day of the flood, "all the fountains of the great deep burst forth, and the windows of the heavens were opened. And rain fell upon the earth forty days and forty nights."[11] Water came from above and from below, like it never had before, and never will again. Noah spends many years preparing for something the world has never seen before, that will come someday. I'm sure people thought Noah was out of his mind.

Seminary was my first Noah moment. I stepped out in faith and obeyed the Lord with this crazy God-given idea to go to graduate school and build a wedding-planning business. I had no idea if or when rain would come or how. I just knew I'd need a "boat" for whatever God had planned. I just said yes and started building, walking, doing, and faith-ing.

The best confirmation to this rapid change of course in my life was that even though the school semester didn't start till September, mandatory orientation for online students began in August. I was standing on campus in August, just like God said, ready for a new adventure. God's direction was clear, in every detail. I had no idea what he had in store for me. In my season at seminary, I was transformed. I was known by myself and others, and brought into a school where Christians from every denomination were welcomed and trained to be spiritual leaders, no matter their past.[12]

---

10 Genesis 6:8-9:17
11 Genesis 7:11-12
12 I make it sound like I was standing at the door of a school for mutant-gifted youngsters. No joke, it kind of felt like that.

God is good at course correction, scary good.

When you're stuck, or seemingly in the wrong place, or it feels like you missed your calling, God loves to jump-start your life in a different direction and lead you back onto the path he planned for you. When we seek him, it's not really possible to miss out on things.

Mistakes are just detours.

Dad saying, "No" so that I would go to UNM, the personal struggles that delayed me until the online program was available, getting the certificate in Wholisitic Kinesiology[13] that led me to that acupuncture table, working for myself so I could have six to eight weeks off every year to travel for seminary—they were all part of God's divine plan. He truly worked all things together for my good.[14] Everything that looked like a messy detour was really just a scavenger hunt for each and every tool I needed.

Had I gone straight into ministry out of high school, I would have been so naïve. I wouldn't be writing this same book for you today. Even a few years ago, this book would have been different. If God didn't send me the long way through the desert, I wouldn't have the wisdom and grace and compassion for myself and others that I need to be a spiritual director. If I didn't go the long way around, I wouldn't have the battle scars and wounds and painful memories that make me relatable, discerning, and compassionate.

Our program wasn't just about theology and education; it was also a personal and spiritual rehabilitation program. Our professors modeled how to walk someone through their spiritual formation by walking us through our own radical reformation. We were made into dust[15] and transformed, reformed, and healed one semester at a time. They helped us see how all our desert wanderings, and all the wanderings of others, were the unique stories that made us beautiful.

---

13 Yes, that's spelled correctly.
14 Romans 8:28
15 Isaiah 30:14

We learned how to pour the gold of heaven's perspective into all our cracks and brokenness. Like spiritual Kintsugi:

> "Kintsugi is the Japanese art of putting broken pottery pieces back together with gold— built on the idea that in embracing flaws and imperfections, you can create an even stronger, more beautiful piece of art. Every break is unique and instead of repairing an item like new, the 400-year-old technique actually highlights the 'scars' as a part of the design. Using this as a metaphor for healing ourselves teaches us an important lesson: Sometimes in the process of repairing things that have broken, we actually create something more unique, beautiful and resilient."[16]

In order to humbly embrace and admit our flaws and weaknesses, we had to give up quite a bit of ego and learn about the "shame gremlins" that hold us back. Leaving seminary, we were more balanced. We didn't think of ourselves as more or less than anyone else. And most importantly, we had studied diversity enough to know we don't know what it's like to be in someone else's experience, and through that perspective, we actually could be outside ourselves just enough to try to walk in their shoes.

Seminary professors led us safely through the spiritual forest so that we could lead others through the forest. They taught us how to read the trail map. If someone walked on a different path than us, we knew how to keep from getting them or ourselves lost. And if they thought they were lost, we knew how to find and reassure them, they were not. God was just leading them into uncharted territory and since he is good and safe, it would all be ok. We are all just following where the Lord leads, and for all of us, that looks different.

Pause.

In case you need to hear this....
You are not lost, friend.

---

16 Tiffany Ayuda, "How the Japanese Art of Kintsugi Can Help You Deal with Stressful Situations," NBCnews.com, April 28, 2018, nbcnews.com/better/health/how-japanese-art-technique-kintsugi-can-help-you-be-more-ncna866471

God has you, no matter how messy life looks.
It will all be OK. Trust him.
He is in the detours.

I also came out of seminary unafraid of asking or being asked big, scary questions. It seemed like every challenge to our faith, our worthiness, or our mission had been asked so that we could stand confidently in ourselves and in our faith. At some point in time, I realized our professor's main goal was to get us to think outside the box. Religion had become a box to contain and explain God. We needed to break outside the box to be more in tune with God and ourselves and creation. I was already pretty good at that. My diverse Christian background was finally to my benefit! Where my peers had black and white rules about what fit and what didn't in their religious tradition, I did not. I would smile and remember Rob Bell, and think, "Yep.[17] It all fits."

Everything good comes from God, and all things are his.[18]

Once, our Old Testament professor asked us what would happen to our theology if there really were aliens. I sat in the back and smiled while I watched my friend's brain pop like popcorn. It was unforgettable. I thought, "What if pastors asked us questions like that on Sunday?" Sure, we'd lose some people. They'd freak out. But, we'd also make quite a few people radically unwavering in their faith. I loved to ask the big and intimidating questions.

My God-box became large and vast and full of curiosity and wonder and I found like-minded people who were also weird and wonderful inside and out. The Quaker-contemplative traditions added exactly what I was missing in my hybrid Christian experience. I exited seminary thinking I knew who I was. I might be a Christian hybrid, but I had met and liked my true self and I was vulnerably known by others and by God. I knew

---

17 In Rob Bell's original *Everything is Spiritual* tour, he used a dry erase marker and a whiteboard to demonstrate that a two dimensional people can't comprehend a three dimensional God pass through their world. He says, "Yep." And his tone is burned in my brain, forever. It's so good. Go watch it. *Everything is Spiritual*. Rob Bell. United States: Zondervan, 2007.
18 James 1:17; Deuteronomy 10:14

how to listen to people's souls, and recognize masks, shame, and authentic vulnerability. I wanted to make sure, on a deep level, people felt understood. I wanted them to know they were loved. I had a mission, or so I thought.

When I graduated, instead of visiting the city of roses every few months, I was back in the New Mexico desert, spiritually and physically. I lost my like-minded faith community. After a season of eye-opening revelations, I returned to life as it was before school. I was still a wedding planner, with weddings booked out for at least another year, and didn't see a cloud in the sky for that "rain" I had predicted years before. I started my spiritual direction business, but with my heavy wedding workload, I really didn't have time to dedicate to it. I had all this internal resistance. I had this underlying belief that people don't pay for spiritual things because they can go to church for free. I felt stuck.

Then one of my friends told me she was connected to these spiritual, soul-centered, business ladies who were leading a retreat. I thought going on a soul-focused business retreat with my friend was exactly what I needed. Even if their spirituality wasn't the same as mine, I was confident I knew how to take what was good and leave the rest. I trusted myself more than I should have.[19]

I had no idea I was walking into a retreat full of shaman rituals, witchcraft, and goddess worship, advertised as self-love, business advice, and being a worker of the light. That retreat, which should have freaked me out, was so shiny and pretty, I didn't see it for what it really was: worshiping money and ego and being taught others knew how to run my business better than I did. They were charismatic and charming, and opened doors to a world I'd never known.

What seemed to be very innocent in my search for direction and wisdom and more of God, hurt me more than it helped. Trusting others to tell me what to do with my business, meant replacing them and their methods with God's direction in my life and my heart. That may sound drastic to you, but it is drastic.

---

[19] Proverbs 16:18; Isaiah 5:21

"The voice you obey is your God."[20]

A foundational, imperative part of being Christian, is loving God first. I had no idea that I was inching towards making their community and circle of thoughts and opinions the loudest voice in my life. I didn't stop spending time with God or stop reading my Bible; I went to church more than once a week. But these experiences somehow silenced God's voice, made me forget who I was, and watered down his word. How could something so seemingly innocent invade my mind so intensely? It was disobeying the first and second commandments, and it placed confidence in the flesh.

In Christianity, we aim to replace our selfish, human, weak "flesh" with the Spirit. We take our fleshly desires, the things we think we want, the cultural expectations we have around success and living a happy life, and we hand it all to the Lord. We choose to say in our hearts, "God, you know what's best for me. I will follow you and put you first so that all that I need and desire will be given to me in your way and in your timing." As we reprioritize our lives to put God first, all the things we need in this life will be given to us.[21]

These coaches said all my success was based on my own striving, my own manifesting, my own work, instead of faith in a good Father to provide and bless me. After a short time, I was more confused,[22] more doubtful, more overwhelmed, and more fearful, and therefore, way less capable of running a business than I was before I started. I was looking for answers anywhere and everywhere when I should have been asking God alone.[23]

After only a short time in this environment, I was not the same woman who walked out of seminary. I was being told to follow my intuition, but I was listening to so many voices that I couldn't discern the outside from my gut or the Holy Spirit. I was trapped in constant self-improvement, which is really just spiritual makeup to cover the lie that you're not enough. I was told I didn't know who I was and that I was finally figuring it out.

---

20 Credit to my pastor of many years, Dr. Alan Hawkins, at New Life City in Albuquerque, NM, for saying this many times. Quoted with permission.
21 Matthew 6:33
22 Deuteronomy 28:20
23 Proverbs 3:5-6

I doubted everything I had ever known.

I had done all the things I thought I should throughout the process. I prayed and asked God to open my eyes and tell me if it wasn't right. I looked for confirmation. I prayed, "God if this isn't of you, if it's not right, if you don't want me to do it, I won't. Take it away from me. Show me!" He let me spiral. He let me walk through a dry desert, but I didn't even know at first, because it was so shiny and glittery there, like a mirage.

When I cried out for help, God answered and rescued me from the pit. Even though I was going through a faith crisis, he came. Even though I didn't even know if Jesus mattered anymore, Jesus came. I was sure everything was spiritual and everything had meaning, but at that point, I wondered if it was just because of aliens. I had stumbled into deconstructing my faith.

Throughout all my doubt and fear and questioning, God stood by my side. He was faithful. While I had been completely confident asking all the big scary questions in seminary, living them out was completely different. I thought I was ready and secure enough to recognize false teaching and be a light in the darkness. I was wrong.

The enemy truly comes as an angel of light.[24] I had never felt so heavy and exhausted, or so full of despair. What began as seemingly innocent and helpful and even fun, now had supernatural power. Evil had come in the side door and only Jesus could kick it out.

God didn't prevent me or warn me. He didn't open my eyes. He let me wander. He let me be blind and deceived until his perfect timing arrived to pull me out. Only through experience could I discern and see the darkness that masqueraded as the light for what it was—the enemy that comes to steal, kill, and destroy while promising to give you the world.[25]

God let me "date the devil" so to speak, so I could have deep experiential knowledge. Jesus knows this. If I knew I was walking away from him, I

---

24 2 Corinthians 11:14
25 Matthew 4:8-9

would have never done it. But after realizing I had wandered into enemy territory, I was the princess who was ready to call out to my prince and ask him to rescue me.

I believe and know from this experience, if you wander away from God, whether you know you're doing it or not, he'll let you. But, he does work all things for good for those who love him.[26] He isn't worried about the results of a bad turn. He might use that detour to expel fear and doubt and lies from your life and give you more discernment, authority, wisdom, and love.

His ways are so much higher than our ways.[27] He sees so much more potential in the process than we do. God *is* the Holy Spirit of Revelation.[28] When we ask to see more and know more, we're asking for more of him and less of us. We can only see what he brings into our awareness. Only God can heal our blindness, and we have to ask for the ability to see and hear and know the way.

Transformation is the answer to the problem of evil in the world. But, walking through a transformation in the spiritual desert is not for the faint of heart. The Bible calls it walking through the refiner's fire or the furnace of affliction.[29] If we are transformed by our experience, then nothing is counted as a total loss. In hindsight, you will find everything had a purpose. There is always something we can learn, always something to be grateful for. Even if it's simply the knowledge we would never go there again, and thankful we survived.

If that feels too radical to you, and something in your life feels too big a loss to be redeemed or healed, I want you to know I've been there. I have been confused by change and unexpected circumstances. I have been deeply wounded by broken promises. I have sobbed on the floor uncontrollably in the fetal position because of overwhelming grief and pain. You are not alone. God's healing and redemption might not look the way we thought it would or come as quickly as we'd wish, but he is the Healer.

---

26 Romans 8:28
27 Isaiah 55:8
28 Ephesians 1:17
29 Isaiah 48:10

God still speaks. He still moves. He is still with you, even in the darkness and suffering. Even when it's so dark, you can't see, he sees and he hears your cry. Do not waste your worship on gods who cannot see and cannot hear; seek the one who listens and sees you.[30]

There is enough redemption here on earth to see that every experience shapes us and makes us who we are. God is for us.[31] No weapon formed against us shall prosper.[32] All our cracks can be filled with gold and made more beautiful. All we have to do is cry out and ask Jesus to heal our broken hearts with his love and fill us with his Spirit. He is faithful and merciful to answer our cries and rescue us, but we have to be honest with ourselves and face our questions and brokenness.

No other person, no other love, would understand that wandering far away will eventually bring us closer. Only Jesus is that patient and that kind. We have to gain experiential knowledge to recognize his way is better than our way. Jesus honors the free will the Father gave us. We all have areas in our life where we are enslaved to fear, anger, addiction, codependency, or doubt. We may not see we are in slavery and captivity to the things that wish to harm and destroy us until we've wandered far away from safety.

Even when we ask God to show us and open our eyes to these things, sometimes he doesn't do it for a long time. Sometimes it feels like I'm running around blind, like a chicken with my head cut off. One of these days, when we are struck with spiritual blindness, maybe we'll wise up, sit, and wait for an answer[33] instead of running around falling in dark holes.[34]

I really do believe everything, even timely blindness, happens for a reason. Walking through the fire or through the darkness is sometimes the only way to break us of our pride and bring us closer to him. Wandering through the desert and stumbling into mirages will remind us that even though we think we know what we're doing, we don't. These searches for the truth

---

30 Deuteronomy 4:28-31
31 Romans 8:31
32 Isaiah 54:17
33 Like Habakkuk, more on this later...
34 Matthew 15:14

build character and humility. They bring us into a deeper love for the Lord, developing our faith and trust in him.

Walking through the darkness, I longed for the light of the world,[35] Jesus, to direct my every step. I longed to be restored by his love.[36]

God knows the end before the beginning.
He knows what we need to get where we're going.
He knows we learn through mistakes and pain.
He knows that distance makes the heart grow fonder.
He knows us better than we know ourselves.
He wants to partner with you on the journey through the desert.
God knows the journey will heal your heart.

Life will shake you. *But if you hold onto God, even while things are shaking, then only the things that are secure in him will remain.* In Revelation 3:18, Jesus says, "I counsel you to buy from me gold refined by fire, so that you may be rich." Walking through difficult life experiences are the way we buy gold. Life shaking us will expose any cracks in our beliefs and our foundation and then (if we let him) God fills those cracks with gold.

We all know the best of people have had the hardest lives. They have been molded and shaped by their experiences and have "hearts of gold."

Whether we choose to get away from God or accidently wander away, when we see how yucky life is without him, how all our worldly desires are unfulfilling, we will return to Him and seek His way with all we have. God doesn't want you to be his robot or zombie. He doesn't want people to be brainless or programmed to be perfect little angels that offer him unemotional love. He wants a dynamic relationship with you. That means he likes you and he loves you. God wants to be an active participant, who is invited, by you, into your life.

The thing with free will is, it's free.

---

35 John 1:1-5
36 Psalm 23

Return to Love

God won't be mad at you for making mistakes. He gave you the free will permission to make them. God won't punish you for making mistakes; he already paid the price for them, and he knows how much you're going to learn. He is always eagerly listening for us to turn away from our captor and towards his love. Even in the midst of falling prey to the same trap over and over again, even when we think we should have known better, he is there, waiting to come to our aid. God will use every mistake to tear away all the things that hinder love, bring you closer to him and to the truth, and open your eyes to see more and more and more, if you ask him.

A couple of invaluable lessons came out of this time walking in the dark. Jesus never left my side. I learned to judge less and love more, and take the responsibility of leadership, especially spiritual direction, very seriously. It made it very clear to me that if I ever have a voice or a platform and I see people looking to me for answers instead of looking to God for answers, then I want to point them to the source, Jesus.

I do not want someone to feel like I have all the answers and I especially do not want people to feel taken advantage of, charmed, manipulated, used, or under a spell. I'm here to invite you deeper into the greatest love story[37] of all time and walk through a part of your life with you. I'm standing at a door, with a sign that says, "The truth is this way." People choose to walk through it, or not.

God has made lots of
> **radical promises**
>> to the people who love Him.

God has promised to love us and his love is not conditional. His love does not fluctuate based on our actions or looks. His love is based on what Jesus did on the cross. Because of that one action, loving us before we loved him[38] by exchanging his life for ours, we are invited into an unconditionally loving relationship. We are always invited to be in communion with God.

---

37 The Bible, the story of Jesus and us.
38 1 John 4:19

He wants a covenant. Covenants are permanent relationships with promises or vows, like marriage, where people build unions and deep relationships based on trust and love, heart and soul, and justice and peace. He wants that with you.

Always.
No matter what you've done.
No matter where you've been.
No matter how worthless or unworthy you feel.
No matter how much you hate him.
No matter who you've slept with.
God will never stop inviting you to be close to him.
We, you, I, just have to believe.

All we do is say, "Yes" to what Jesus did for us,
and ask him to fill us with his Spirit.

Jesus compared God to a Vinedresser. He said God sharpens and shapes and prunes us. He understands that some growth happens simply for the purpose of pruning back. And when we fall and cry out for help, he picks us up and reattaches us to his life source, just like branches are grafted into a vine. He's promised to do this for those who abide in his love.[39]

This is the foundational reason why after studying almost all the world's religions (including some by accident), I continue to choose Christianity. I have found Christianity to be the only faith system that doesn't teach, "You can do it." When I look around at our world, it's clear we have no idea what we're doing. When you get to the core of every religion, they all seem to say if you work hard enough, you can reach your end goal. They're all based on pride, way deep down.

Christianity is the only faith system that says we will continue to mess up no matter how hard we try. No matter how much we strive or desire to be good, we will fall short. God is perfect and we cannot be perfect. We can be good by our worldly standards. We can compare ourselves to others and say

---
[39] Luke 11:9-13; Jeremiah 29:12

we're better than so-and-so because he did something worse than we did in life, but we will never be able to compare ourselves to Jesus and still call ourselves good. We are filthy next to a perfect God until he washes us clean.

We need Jesus.
We can't do it alone.
We need Divine intervention.

Christianity says God created you for communion and togetherness. Christianity says you can't do it alone, in your own power or your own strength. You were literally made to love God and be loved by him. You will always feel incomplete and unsatisfied in life until you give up trying to do things your way and looking for love in all the wrong places.

We were made for a relationship with the God who is love. We are truly incomplete without Jesus; we need him. He sees the potential that other people do not. He is the Healer, who brings truth and justice to all the lies, accusations, and shame. We need his healing, his freedom, and his peace. We need his love and mercy. When we surrender to his love and his way by putting him first, God will take care of everything else.

Even crazier than a God who does all the work for us, who died for us, who desires to be with us, who is ready and willing to rescue us from ourselves at any given moment, God even takes the responsibility of growing in love for him off our shoulders. God doesn't even ask us to work to transform ourselves or grow in love for him. All we have to do is agree with his way, make a choice to love him, and ask. He just says, "Say yes to me and ask of me, and I will generously give."

He's inviting us to ask for a desire to love him more.
He's inviting us to cry out when we're trapped and held captive by the things that hold us back.
He's inviting us to ask for his help to draw near to him and wander less.
He's inviting us to hand over our hearts to be healed and filled with his Spirit.
He's inviting us to be transformed into the light of the world.

He's inviting us to ask him to remove everything that hinders love.
He's asking you to wander the desert with him, searching for gold.

He will do *all* of life with you.
All you have to do is ask.

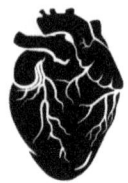

Invitation to Prayer

Lord, Thank you for all the detours.
You are so good and so holy. You know exactly where I'm going and I do not.
Thank you that you go before me and you know that I need experiential knowledge in order to walk the way you want me to walk.
Thank you that you are trustworthy and a Good Shepherd who leads me with wisdom and mercy. Thank you that you have created an epic adventure for us to live together.

Show me what I learned in the hard seasons.
Show me the experiential knowledge I needed and the tools you put in my tool belt to prepare me for what's next.
I'm sorry for all the times I kicked and screamed and resisted your way and your love. I'm sorry for all the temper tantrums and tears, for begging you to change my circumstances and do things my way.
I believe you know where we're headed and exactly what I need to get there.
When I reflect on your patience and kindness,
I stand in awe of your divine wisdom.

Put in me a heart that longs to be close to you.
Put in me a desire to know and love you more. I'm asking you to remove all the things that stand in my way of loving you first,
of living out the greatest commandments.

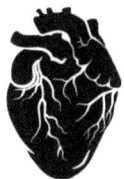

Please open my eyes to see when I'm starting to wander away from your will or your way. Prevent me from being distracted by mirages; lead me not into temptation.
Convict me, purify me, and call me. Turn my heart towards you, Lord.

Jesus, thank you for coming into this big, beautiful world and experiencing the pain and suffering of being human. I know you are not a God who is distant and does not understand me. I know you intimately experienced the pain of living on Earth and know what it's like to be tempted when you're at your weakest.

Thank you for choosing the Father's way over your own way, even when tempted, so I could be close to you and abide in you. Thank you that you are always with me and never forsake me.
I do not want to belittle the cross by continuing to sin as I please. Come and rescue me from all the things that hold me captive, whether I'm aware of them or not. I know you hear and see all things, even into my heart. Have mercy on me and lead me into the light.

I do want to be a light in the world. Thank you for loving me.
Amen.

Human Rollercoasters

The Bible is full of all the best stories. The characters are real and relatable and full of drama. It really is better than a soap opera.

The Bible doesn't get enough credit for being dramatic because it is concise. It often tells us the facts, therefore, it doesn't always express the emotional turmoil the characters went through as they chose to obey the Lord. It doesn't explain how the Lord intervening caused chaos in their hearts, minds, and lives.

Our journey with Jesus can feel like a rollercoaster of ups and downs. Many assume that when we give our lives over to God, everything will be easier. It is, but not in the way we assume. It's not like all our problems go away and our loved ones start caring more and communicating better overnight. Instead, we have a partner who is with us. Whether high or low, *we're not alone.*

When I was roughly fourteen, Jesus appeared to me in a vision. This is the life-altering experience I mentioned earlier. I was at a youth conference and I saw him on the cross right in front of me. It was just like you read about in ancient or mystic stories. I know I was in a large auditorium with hundreds of other kids my age, but I had a vision that was so real, it was as if Jesus transported through time to meet me. I saw him on the cross, right before my very eyes. He told me he loved me and he died for me, and he loved the world and died for the world.[1] He said, "Tell the world I love them and died for them."

I wept and wept on the floor, overcome by how much he loved us all. Every day after, I felt compelled[2] to tell everyone how much he loved them. Not in a gross, pushy, bible-thumping evangelical way. In a deep, moving, heartfelt, personal, "Don't you see how beautiful he is?" kind of way. I felt drawn to him. That mystical moment is more real to me than reality. Ever since then, something has been missing. Heaven touched earth, and I witnessed it, and that taste never leaves you.

I'll be honest. In some seasons, I ignored the longing and distracted myself with life. Sometimes I tried to fill it with other things, wishing the instant gratification would be enough. But, when I'm in tune with myself and honest, it's like the world isn't right without him here. I miss him like a widow misses the love of her life. My long-lost love died for the whole world, and my heart wants him here with us. It longs for the people around me to know him too.

As you've heard, I spent my life getting as close as I could. I studied the Bible, Jesus, the Holy Spirit, prayer, the Father's heart, all the while trying to seek and find the man who appeared to me. I studied world religions and found the ways the rest of the world thinks of God, and some of the ways the enemy harms, steals, and destroys[3] people through mocking and mimicking the one true God.

The more I get to know him and learn about him, the more I am fascinated by him and his ways. This unboxable God will forever expand your mind and perspective if you let him. He is so good and so mysterious. He is gracious and compassionate, slow to anger, and rich in love.[4] You will never run out of new things to see.

---

1 John 3:16
2 1 Corinthians 9:16
3 John 10:10
4 Psalm 145

Human Rollercoasters || 53

I look at the Earth, and the crazy people in it, and wonder why he created us all. I wonder, more specifically, why he gives us so much freedom to mess things up. I see the hurting and the poor and the rich and the wicked. I hear him say again, "I love them."

Sometimes, his ways make no sense.
But, love can be like that.
Love is more ethereal and less logical than we'd prefer.

I see the beautiful ocean and mountains and go for long drives to listen to worship music and praise him for the stars and all the things he created for us to enjoy, and then read in the Bible that it's all going to be destroyed. I'm in awe and tremble at this jealous and righteous king who knows what it will take for arrogant and stubborn people to turn to Him and his leadership. It is in kindness that he lets us discover that we ruin things and simply can't live our best life without him.[5]

That's what this relationship is all about—*choosing to love him and have faith in his way, no matter what the world around us looks like.*

We would all prefer that sin and suffering be eradicated from the earth, and eventually it will be. That's a promise Christians hold onto; Jesus is coming back to make the wrong things right. The prophecies of the second coming of Jesus have yet to be fulfilled. How and when they will be fulfilled, we have no idea. The Bible says not even Jesus knows the time of his return.[6]

One of the things that always stands out to me when reading the Bible is that all the Old Testament prophecies written about Jesus only make sense to us now, because He came and fulfilled them. We can see them now that they have been fulfilled. When we read a prophecy such as, "He was pierced for our transgressions,"[7] now knowing Jesus was crucified for our sins, we connect the two. But before he came to fulfill it, there is no way the people or the prophets knew exactly how the story would unfold. The last thing

---

[5] We are the ones destroying our planet, and we need God's wisdom to steward it and care for it.
[6] Mark 13:32; Matthew 24:36
[7] Isaiah 53:5

people would have guessed was that God was going to come down to our level embodying human flesh and let us kill him on a cross.

How could God,
    who is so holy,
        take on the form of man,
            and voluntarily
                put himself through the most excruciating
    and humiliating death known in all of history?
What God could be so humble?
    Only Yeshua Hamaschiach;
            Jesus Christ.

Jesus chose to love us, even when it cost him his life. No other religion reflects a God who serves humans. In every religion, people have to work to please the gods, we have to strive and beg them for all our needs. The Hebrew-Christian God is radically counter-cultural. In fact, the way of the I AM is so upside-down and backwards to our natural instincts, that we can only understand it with Divine help.

We are all doing the best we can with the knowledge we have. We all do what is right in our own eyes,[8] but only God knows the truth. Only God sees the heart of our actions. He sees everything, even our blindness. Even more so, as the God that sees, he's in charge of our sight. He reveals truth and sight to us as he divinely chooses. Knowing the Father was in charge of the sight of the people, Jesus prays from the cross. "Father, forgive them, for they know not what they do."[9] Jesus had compassion on the people because he knew how blind and helpless they were.[10]

Throughout the Bible, there is a theme of needing "eyes to see and ears to hear."[11] Many generations and many people have, throughout history, lacked sight and hearing for the truth. Today we are still limited by our own sight and must pray for the "Spirit of wisdom and of revelation"[12]

8 Proverbs 21:2
9 Luke 23:34
10 Matthew 9:36
11 Deuteronomy 29:4; Ezekiel 12:2; Matthew 11:15; any many other places.
12 Ephesians 1:17

to know God and his ways. We must ask to have "the eyes of our hearts enlightened."[13] We are in desperate need.

However, even this prayer does not come with instant revelation. Our transformation is always on God's timeline. Sadly the moment we're confident in our sight is often the moment we fulfill the unavoidable truth that pride and arrogance come before a fall.[14]

The Lord gives us free will, and our choices make us who we are. We can choose to make God the Lord and leader of our life, or all the other voices vying for our attention. God is not afraid of the competing voices.

God let the religious leaders, who were blind guides, lead the blind populous into fear and accusations. God used their hard hearts and religious rules and blindness to create a path for Jesus to the cross. In order for the will of God to be fulfilled, there had to be a group of people that were blind and arrogant enough to crucify Jesus.

God didn't kill Jesus. People are given free will to murder, and they did.

They chose to follow the popular, loud, authoritative voices, instead of standing up to defend the way, the truth, life. Jesus was the embodiment of holiness, the light of the world. They chose religion's way over God's way. They chose darkness over light. They chose to put religion in power by obeying and heeding those voices, instead of God's voice. They chose fear and pride and murder over truth and peace and love.

It wasn't God's will that his son would die on a cross. It was his will that Adam and Eve would trust his direction back in the garden, but they didn't. It was his will that he would love us, no matter the cost. No matter how we treated him or his son. No matter how much we run away, spit on him, mock him, beat him, it was and is his will to fully submit to us in self-sacrificial love, even to the point of death. God will give us the desires of our hearts, even if it breaks his. He pays the price for all of our free-will choices.

---

13 Ephesians 1:18
14 Proverbs 16:18

God is too good to not use our own blindness for our own good. The High Priest of the day, Caiaphas, is recorded saying to the council of chief priests and Pharisees, "You know nothing at all. Nor do you understand that it is better for you that one man should die for the people, not that the whole nation should perish."[15] Caiaphas didn't know what he was saying. The council was concerned the Roman empire would come to squash them because Jesus was causing waves; Caiaphas had no idea his prophetic utterance had another meaning, that Jesus would be able to die as the sacrificial lamb, not only for Israel, but for the world.

It's a hard teaching, an intense and difficult and humbling reality, to accept that our blindness could be used for a purpose and maybe even play a role in fulfilling God's bigger plan. It's a very backwards way of thinking, to say God knew what that evil generation would do, and he sent Jesus anyway. God knew that humans were so blind to true love and set in their ways, that they would kill Jesus to avoid change. Selfish men who cared more about their own political and religious agenda over God's agenda killed Jesus. But God was and is not surprised. He planned to use their evil plans for good all along.

Even Jesus' disciples, who were the closest to him, did not understand what Jesus meant when he told them directly that he would die and rise again. It was so far outside their understanding, that even though he told them directly, bluntly, exactly what would happen, they didn't get it. "This saying was hidden from them, and they did not grasp what was said."[16]

Israel was not looking for a messiah who would die. They were looking for a military conqueror who would overthrow Roman rule and avenge them from their oppressors. This is what they had been taught their whole lives. This is how their religious leaders had interpreted the scripture. They were narrow sighted, looking with their physical eyes at their physical problems. God wanted to cleanse their spirits and heal their spiritual, eternal lives. God cares more about our eternal life then our temporary experience.

---

15 John 11:49-50
16 Luke 18:34

So then, what would a good and holy God do for a people he loves, even when they misunderstand and hate him in return? How does a kind and patient King rule the Earth while it's full of people who resist him at every turn?

First, he flips their world upside down by showing them who he really is, not who they interpreted him to be. He dies for their resistance and hatred, to tear the wall between the human soul and God, so that individuals no longer need a middle man or religion, but instead, can worship and seek him in spirit and truth from anywhere, all the time. Then he sends the Holy Spirit to guide his people and be with them in all they do.

Anyone who asks and believes can experience the kingdom of God in their daily lives. Most of the world doesn't know that truth, not even Christians. God gave us the answer to love and freedom. His name is Jesus. But barely anyone knows because people who claim Christianity have given it such a bad reputation. They have just put new names on the old system that Jesus came and died to change.

We can't continue on this way. We need God's help. Our world is overflowing with evil hearts, debased minds, and people pursuing their own selfish desires, not caring who they harm in the process. We are in a world full of narcissists and victims. We are a world full of blind guides claiming to be woke, but more asleep than ever before.

Let's stop searching for love in all the wrong places.
Let's seek God's heart instead.
Let's try doing things God's way.
Jesus and his disciples said just that,
"Repent, for the kingdom of heaven is at hand."[17]

It's *here*.
Now.
It's within arm's reach.

---

[17] Matthew 4:17

Hold out your hand and ask for God to open your eyes and bring you into his kingdom reality, now.

The basic directions for everyone to enter the kingdom is the same: repent, and say yes to love. Believe Jesus died for you and rose again and choose to follow him. Love God with all your heart, mind, and strength. Ask the Holy Spirit to come into you and guide you. But for each and every one of us, the specifics of what hinders growth in that relationship is different. The only way to know is to talk to God about it. When we ask the Lord what stands in the way, his answer could be out of left field. It might not at all be what we would expect.

Take Abraham for example. Abraham's story is a story of faith, patience, and being willing to give up what we love most for the Lord. Abraham's story is so relatable. When we look at his story, we would say Abraham rides a rollercoaster of faith. He has hope and faith when God speaks, and he acts quickly to obey the direct commands of the Lord without much resistance. But when the Lord is quiet, Abraham wanders around through life, making all kinds of mistakes.

Despite the highs and lows, God says Abraham did not waver.[18] While he might have been going up and down emotionally, feelings are not facts. Deep in his soul, Abraham must have believed God could, at any time, do what he said he would do. We can learn from witnessing his struggle and his relationship with the Lord, and we can learn how God sees us, even when we feel like we're going up and down.

If you do not know the story, before God changed their names to Abraham and Sarah, Abram and Sarai lived with his Dad. The story begins by telling us that the Lord speaks to seventy-five year old Abram and tells him to leave his father's home and go to a land God will show him. God tells him he's going to make a great nation out of Abram and he will bless him so greatly that all the families of the Earth will be blessed because of him.

The next line in the Bible is, "So Abram went."[19]

18 Romans 4:20-21
19 Genesis 12:4

It's a little crazy to think he just got up and left. The older I get, the more sure I am when God speaks, because I become more familiar and recognize the many ways He speaks: in gut feelings, in whispers, in dreams or pictures, through direct words, or through others. Abram must have had a lifetime of hearing the Lord and building a relationship with him in order to pack up his life and travel to literally only God knows where. Abram must have been sure.

The first place they come to, God speaks. He says, "to your offspring I will give this land."[20] But, Abram builds an altar to the Lord and moves on. It's kind of weird. We don't really know why Abram kept traveling. Maybe Abram thought when God said, "to your offspring," he thought the word was only for the future and not for him, now. Maybe he wasn't welcomed by the current occupants.

Either way, as is typical of life, things take an unexpected turn for the worst. Famine hits the land, and they have to go to Egypt for provision. If the story wasn't weird already, Abram turns to his apparently gorgeous wife and basically says "Babe, you're so beautiful. When we get to Egypt, those thugs are going to kill me so they can have you for themselves. Don't tell them you're my wife. Tell them you're my sister, so they don't kill me." Sure enough, the local men see Sarai and he was right, they think she's gorgeous. She's taken into Pharaoh's house, and Abram is given a large bride price. After a white lie (Sarai was technically his half-sister) and putting her in a precarious situation, God blesses the socks off him.

What a strange story.

The man who left his Dad's house in a heartbeat when told he would be made into a great nation, now fears an early death, prior to having any children. From our perspective, not only does Abram selfishly put his life above his wife's purity and honor, he also doesn't seem to consider Sarai's role as an important part of the Lord's promise to have children. He's a typical, patriarchal male. He interprets God's word through his worldview.

---

[20] Genesis 12:7

Return to Love

Thank God, God doesn't think like Abram or us. God is about defending the vulnerable. He has his eye on Sarai. When Abram doesn't protect his wife, God steps in for her. God sends plagues to Pharaoh and his house because of Sarai. As soon as Pharaoh realizes Sarai is the cause of the plagues, he confronts Abram. "How could you do this to me? Why didn't you tell me she was your wife!?" Pharaoh gives him his wife back and kicks him out of the country.

It seems to me Abram could have been in more danger pissing off Pharaoh than he ever was by just having a beautiful wife. But he leaves, "very rich in livestock, in silver, and in gold."[21] He has so much, it causes strife within his family, and the conflict makes him separate from his nephew to keep the peace.

Possibly unsure where to go next, Abram returns to the place where he last heard the voice of the Lord. It's where God said "to your offspring I will give this land." Sure enough, the Lord speaks when he arrives and says look around, all this is going to be yours. It will all belong to your offspring. So, Abram pops up a tent and settles down.

After a while, there is a war going on nearby, and he finds out from his allies that his nephew has been taken captive. He grabs his men and defeats the king's army and rescues Lot, his nephew, and all his belongings. Now, the same man who was afraid to die because of Sarai, is fearless in war.

Do you see the rollercoaster of ups and downs?
Of faith and doubt?

Time passes, and Abram still has no heir. Abram asks the Lord about being childless. God assures Abram he will have an heir. God says to consider the stars and the sand. He says Abram's offspring will be innumerable like these. He tells him things that will happen to his offspring many generations later, and he makes a covenant with Abram that all his promises will be fulfilled.

---

[21] Genesis 13:2

Human Rollercoasters | 61

After such an intense download from the Lord, I'm sure Abram was feeling pretty confident again. So let's get super real. Abram comes home from sleeping in the field, very excited, and declares, "The Lord told me we're going to have a baby!"

This is not the first time Sarai has heard this.

She's probably not excited about this at all. She has to try all over again, and feel all the disappointment again, and experience the hope and grief again when she sees other babies in their community. She probably feels like it's her fault they can't get pregnant. Proverbs says, "Hope deferred makes the heart sick."[22] The lack of fulfillment in a promise like this is the ultimate hope deferred. Sarai's heart is probably in incredible emotional pain over not having a child.

Abram's rollercoaster is also Sarai's rollercoaster. This word from the Lord, that should bring hope and joy to a couple, is probably the biggest burden in their marriage. When he shows up with renewed hope, she knows what that means: there are going to be a lot of nights trying to make a baby. And it will quickly switch from enjoyment to no longer being fun. It will turn into a burden, because their physical relationship is not the enjoyment of intimacy, it's a means to an end. It's probably been tearing them apart for years. It probably creates doubt and resentment.

Clearly, I'm extrapolating. Which, with the Bible, isn't always a smart thing to do. We don't want to read between the lines too much and make up things that aren't really there. That's dangerous territory. However, connecting to these characters and trying to put ourselves in their shoes, requires asking what they could have been feeling and experiencing, and we don't do that enough. Too many people read these stories with detached interest instead of letting themselves feel and connect to the pain and loss the characters felt as they tried to hold onto their faith and obey the Lord. They waited many long years for his promises to come to fruition.

---

22 Proverbs 13:12

My point here in pondering Sarai's thoughts is to encourage you to stop and smell the roses. It's easy to read for information or for the piety of reading instead of actually letting the story sink into your bones and shape you and your life through curiosity and wonder. It would be just as sacrilegious to consider it fantasy. These stories are the experiences of real people with real pain and real joy. These stories tell us how to live, how to be shaped by God, how humans are beautifully broken and redeemed in this world God created, and how he walked with them in their unique journey. These stories are full of limitless depth. Both God and the Bible are infinitely bigger and deeper and more profound than we can uncover in our lifelong search.

With that lens, do you see how the Lord intervening in their lives could have brought emotional turmoil and pressure to their relationship?

This isn't a joyful promise anymore.... Sure, it would have been great if it was true the first time around. They entertained the idea for a while, but Sarai's almost seventy-five and Abram's almost eighty-five years old and sex might not be as fun as it used to be.

At this point in the story, they have been trying to have a baby for about ten years. When you think about that environment, years and years of emotional and spiritual turmoil, what Sarai does next doesn't seem as crazy as it sounds. She looks at her young Egyptian servant who is of childbearing age and says to Abram, "Why don't you go marry her and get her pregnant instead?"

The story says, "Abram listened to the voice of Sarai."[23]

Uh oh.

Sarai sees a way out. She sees a way that the word of the Lord can fit within her own understanding, a way that what God said can be fulfilled easily instead of miraculously. There is a way it can be fulfilled now, instead of exercising faith and patience.

---

23 Genesis 16:2

When you're living in the season of heartache and pain, it's really hard to pull yourself outside the emotion. It's difficult to look from a perspective of hope with faith and patience. Abram probably wants his happy wife and happy life back, and he's been given permission to marry and enjoy a younger woman. Of course, he says yes!

The challenge to listen to the voice of the Lord and make his voice more influential in our lives than even that of our family or spouse, is real. When Abram listens to Sarai, he's going outside the covenant relationship the promised child was offered within and seeks to make the word of the Lord come true within the limits of their own understanding. The consequence of this choice is one of the world's biggest conflicts still today. What felt like a logical and practical choice, to both of them, caused more problems than they could have ever fathomed.

Things are going pretty well for about thirteen years. Until God appears to Abram again. "I am God Almighty; walk before me, and be blameless, that I may make my covenant between me and you, and may multiply you greatly."[24]

Abram falls on his face.
I would fall on my face too if the Lord showed up and appeared before me and said be blameless.
How?!
He probably dropped in fear and trembling!

God declares, three times, that Abram will be the father of many nations. God changes his name, from Abram, meaning high or exalted father, to Abraham, father of nations. He changes Sarai, meaning princess, to Sarah, meaning mother of nations. He will bless **her.**

God reminds Abraham of the covenant to him and his offspring and the promise of the land his descendants will occupy. He also gives him specific instructions of what to do in the physical, in order to receive and do his part in making these things come true: go be circumcised.

---

[24] Genesis 17:1-2

All this backstory was to lead you right here. After twenty-four years since the initial word, God tells him what to do for the promise to come true. It's not a command to make this prophecy happen in his own power. It's not a command to go to sleep with his wife. It's a command to cut the excess and unnecessary skin from his most private place, the place directly involved in taking part in intimacy and reproduction. It's a powerful symbol and action to humble himself in this way.

To Abraham's credit, he immediately goes and circumcises himself and every male in his house. He rushes to obey the Lord. He is eager to remove what God says stands in the way of this promise coming true. Not what he, himself thinks stands in the way. He gives up trying to figure things out and do things his way. He opens himself up to receive a miracle. He performs a prophetic act, based on faith alone.

The thing with miracles is they're not miracles unless they are impossible without God's intervention. What is too hard for man is possible for the Lord. If we can do it in our own strength, we can take the credit and wonder if the Lord really did it, or if we did it ourselves. When we reach our breaking point and give up and quit and something comes to pass anyway, God gets all the credit.

We can search all day long for what stands in the way of us experiencing signs and wonders, loving God more, or our prayers being answered, but only God knows. When we pray for a child to return home and stop doing drugs, or for a loved one to return to sound mind, or for healing, or provision, or a child to be born, we only see one way for that path to unfold. That one way is the way of our understanding, bound by our four-dimensional experience. God is not bound by his creation. He is outside of time and space and matter, and yet continues to meet us and work within our limited parameters. We need eyes to see the possibilities outside our limitations and understanding, and at least to be friends with the One who sees it all.

Where our understanding ends, spirituality begins. At the limits of our knowledge, is faith. Faith begins with believing something we don't yet see.

Human Rollercoasters | 65

We can't see the wind, but we see the wind moving trees and leaves. We feel the breeze on our faces. We have enough proof to believe in the invisible, wind. When it's windy outside, and the trees are really rocking, people say, "Do you see the wind?" It's not counterintuitive to believe in the wind or talk about seeing the wind, even though you can't see it, because its effect on the world is obvious.

To those who can see the effects of the Lord on the world, his existence is obvious. To those who can feel him, we have enough proof. *But blessed are those of you who have not seen or heard and still believed.*[25]

I don't know why the Lord chooses to reveal himself to some in ways that others never get to experience. When we look back at the story of Noah, it says that Noah found favor in the eyes of God.[26] I wish it told us how. It seems to be that the world was wicked and Noah set himself apart from that world to seek God. I believe Noah wanted to be a friend of God, and saw that the ways of the world were foolish. I bet he was curious and quiet, a man who kept to himself, and believed when God told him it would rain, that it would rain. I think God and Noah built their relationship over time, and his faith caught God's attention.

This is the paradox of Christianity. Faith is what makes one righteous in the eyes of God, not perfection. God seems to be more understanding of our human depravity than we are. When we strive to obey God's law and be perfect, we fail. When we choose to love him, and ask for his help, we give our hearts willingly and open up to him. Love leads to a natural desire for relationship, obedience and submission to his way. Legalism does not lead to love and commitment.

Months after I heard the Lord say he wanted me to get married again, he officially ushered that man who I heard him say was "the one," into my life. Normally, when you fall in love, something just happens to you. Chemistry and butterflies and excitement take over. It's natural. For me and this guy, things didn't "click" like that. Our relationship felt like we had all the

---

25 John 20:29
26 Genesis 6:8

ingredients to bake a cake but none of the tools. We had no bowl and no spoon to contain or mix all our ingredients properly. Something was missing. After a few short months, we parted ways.

This detour in my life, raised all kinds of tough questions that challenged some of my deepest-held beliefs. Hearing God say something would happen, and me interpreting it a certain way, and then watching my interpretation of his word start to come true, but then crumble, was confusing. It challenged my belief in God's goodness. It made me doubt my ability to hear him speak or understand him. It made me question whether or not I could trust others who had confirmed my understanding. It made me wonder where God's directions end and where he defers to our desires or preferences. In other words, it made me ask a lot of questions about free will. It made me wonder if God withholds his power at the edge of our free will.

Just when I thought I had finished deconstructing, I was facing round two. It took me over a year to heal. Trusting that God led me through that season for a reason, took time. Leaning into faith, believing in his goodness, even when I could not understand how this mess could be "good," was not easy. Believing that he was trustworthy and faithful in the midst of the mess, and that it truly was him that spoke even when it didn't come true, took deep soul searching.

Here is the crazy part. Once I faced all those questions head-on, instead of being bitter or angry, I was overflowing with faith and love. While the physical experience made no sense to me or anyone else, what had happened within me was undeniable.

I learned to be committed and dedicated and sincere in the hard times. I became confident that being in love meant serving someone and putting them first. I felt the selflessness of being willing to die for someone you didn't really know. I tasted what true love was.

I learned how to have faith even when things were at their worst. Like Abraham, I believed what God said was true. I believed he could do it, even when I couldn't see any sign in the physical world that those things would come to pass. Like Noah, I saw potential for rain when there was no cloud in sight. I believed every promise of the Lord again, with fervor, even if free will changed the course of this one coming true.

If that wasn't enough, somehow, miraculously, I had actually fallen in love with God, the matchmaker himself. I loved Jesus more than ever, as if my eyes were opened to see how good he was for the first time. I was excited to partner with God, who wanted me to constantly grow as much as possible, and continually celebrated my success.

Don't get me wrong, it didn't take away the longing for the right man, or the desire to grow old with someone. It didn't make me give up on hope for a best friend to build a life with, raise a family with, or make decisions with. It just made me realize that man has big shoes to fill, because now, counterfeit love couldn't compete with the true love I had tasted. I had spent my life, like all of us, searching for love, but didn't really know what I was looking for.

Bankers don't study fake bills to recognize counterfeits, they study real currency to identify the real thing. When you know what's real, anything that tries to masquerade as the real thing, doesn't fool you.

Somehow, miraculously, this detour showed me Jesus, and I learned to recognize him. Counterfeit love could not compare, and couldn't pass for the real thing anymore. It happened to me so naturally, I didn't even know it was happening...like falling in love.

Once I realized how I had been transformed, I was like a giddy school girl whenever I talked about it. It was embarrassing. I was way too happy to be single in my thirties.

I couldn't help but glow. People would ask me how I was doing and they'd assume we were back together, but I would share about tears at the beach, a car accident, and returning a wedding dress. They were confused. The rollercoaster looked down, but I was up. I felt lighter, and they could see it.

I was confident in myself and my path; I felt satisfied. I had traded fake love for true love, and seen the lover of my soul heal my heart and meet me in my painful circumstances.

Like Abraham's circumcision, I never would have guessed that was the thing to do. I didn't know trusting God with my heart, and having it broken, would be the way to make it whole again. I didn't know that was the experience I needed to remove excess "flesh" from my heart, so I could love him and others wholeheartedly. I didn't see, until then, how I made choices out of perceived obligation and legalism instead of desire and zeal.

In the book of Romans, Paul talks about a "circumcision of the heart."[27] He says our hearts must be circumcised by the Spirit. Only the Lord can cut away the parts of our heart that stand in the way of loving him wholeheartedly because he's the only one that knows what needs to be cut. He longs to hold us where we are, clean us up, and then take us where we were created and designed to go.

"I know how that heart is supposed to look, and that overgrown hardness is hurting its ability to function properly." Who better than the Creator and Great Physician who made it, to say so?

Only he sees, and only he knows what stops us from being passionately, wholeheartedly engaged in life. I didn't know my heart had grown hard from divorce. It was normal to me. I was functioning just fine. But I wasn't thriving.

This world is so full of pain and hurt. Our pain is so normal to us, we don't even feel it. We think the ups and downs of life are normal. We think the rollercoaster is the only way to live until he gently guides us elsewhere. We don't know the life that's available to us, if only we'd ask.

God is so in love with you, that just one glance at him, captivates his heart.[28] Your love is enough. It's all he wants. He wants you. He likes you and he loves you. He wants to live life with you, and grow old with you. He wants to

---

27 Romans 2:29
28 Song of Solomon 4:9

be recognized by your side, day and night.

When we have a relationship with God that's akin to a life partner, we trust him to take care of us. We trust him to act and defend us. We trust him to provide and follow through. We trust him to fulfill his words and promises. When we trust him, we're confident that he loves and desires us even when we're human; indeed, because we're human. The rollercoaster of life does not disqualify us from giving or receiving love.

When we love him, we know even if we make a wrong choice, or miss a turn, he will recalibrate our navigation and give us a detour with a scenic view. The detour might not be painless, but it will be worthwhile. God will act on your behalf. If it's meant to be, you can't miss it. God won't let anything, even our mistakes, interfere with His plans for us, if we ask. All we have to do is give him is our love; he takes care of everything else. *All you have to do is ask.*

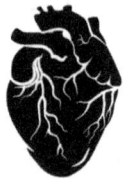

Invitation to Prayer

Lord, I want to love you.
I believe you love me, and I want to love you back. Circumcise my heart and heal the pain and the ups and downs so I can love you with my whole heart. I want to love you, myself, and those around me with a love full of faith and trust. I don't want to lean on my own understanding. Renew a childlike wonder in me. Show me the life that's available to me. Open my eyes to all the possibilities and potential I can't see yet.

Renew my childlike curiosity and wonder.
I want to see how you work on behalf of those who love you and enjoy the journey. Let me see and know your character. Let me see who you really are, not what the world thinks or says about you. I don't want to interpret you through my worldview. I want to see the real you.
Please, expand my God-box.

If there is anything stopping me from believing you love me, remove it for me. I want to overflow with love and stand confidently before you, knowing you are gracious and abounding in steadfast love for me and the world around me.

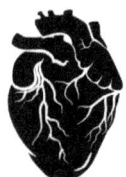

Help me to know what Hosea 6:6 means: that you desire love, not sacrifice. Remove legalism and religious obligations from me, replace them with truth, love, and faith.

Jesus, I'm putting you in the driver's seat.
I trust you to keep me on the path you desire for me, and I give up my fear and worry that we will miss a turn. I place my life in your hands. I trust you with the detours. I trust you to follow through.

Have your way with my heart. You know how it's supposed to look. I trust you as the Great Physician and Healer. I trust you with my destiny, and I trust you will help me let go of everything that doesn't serve my highest purpose. I want to live my very best life. I want to be excited and full of joy and passion. I need and want your fresh breath to breathe on all the dead parts of my life and bring them back to life.
I have faith in your process, in your perfect leadership.
I stand in agreement with your perfect timing.

Do a wondrous work, Lord.
Your will, your way, your timing.
Amen.

Worthy of Love

In a day and age where we try to prove ourselves and build a resume of accolades on social media, it is much easier to focus on what others think of us than what God thinks of us. When we have built a resume and reputation, we think we know what we deserve. We believe we are justified in our expectations of honor and respect. If we don't have the experience society respects (or even if we do), we might have the opposite problem. Rather than arrogance, we struggle with self-hatred and false humility. Unable to receive love, our hearts are buried in shame and unworthiness.

In both giving and receiving, love requires vulnerability. The fear and pain of rejection is what makes us run away from the truth. If we give someone more than they deserve, we could be taken advantage of, and if we receive, we could truly fall in love and we risk our hearts being broken. Rejection and pride in both forms is what makes us shy away from telling the whole truth or our whole story.

We all wrestle internally with our worthiness because of where we've been. We don't typically list our pain and struggles and failures on a resume, but experiential knowledge is exactly what we need to lead others through hardship. It's those very afflictions we think make us unworthy of love and affection that add the gold into our story. Your experiences shaped you into who you are today; and all those scars make you beautiful. You are worthy of love.

Gaining factual knowledge is as easy as searching online. Anyone can tell you the facts or memorize something. Knowledge is not the same as wisdom. The wisdom that comes from experience teaches us that what looks bad could actually be good, and what looks good could actually be bad. We are quick to judge others and be hard on ourselves for our messy detours, but the Lord sees the beauty in our mess. He knows we are a work in progress.

In the movie "The Shack," there is a scene where the main character, Mack, is gardening with the character representing the Holy Spirit. As Mack is digging, he runs into a root that is poisonous. The Holy Spirit warns him to be careful. Alarmed, he asks why something so dangerous would be in the garden. It seems obvious to him that poison is bad. Instead, the Holy Spirit tells him the poison, combined with a flower that was within arm's reach, has incredible healing properties. He looks around and sees a mess, but she looks around, and says it's "wild, wonderful, and perfectly in process."[1]

God is able to see the good in the bad and the bad in the good. What is darkness to us is light to him.[2] He sees our wild, wonderful, messy lives, and understands the time and the season we're in. He sees our potential. He does not fear or hide the poison. He knows the poison, in the right dose, in the right recipe, is not poison at all. It's a catalyst for healing. He knows everything has a purpose, and he sees the beauty in our mess.

In God's eyes, nothing disqualifies you from receiving his love. No "poison" is too great. The blood of Jesus, shed on the cross, is the antidote. He says you are worthy of love and nothing can change that. He knows the wisdom and experience you gained or will gain on your journey. He paid for your mistakes on the cross and nothing you do would stop him from dying for you. *If this God who created us, deemed us worthy of love, who are we to argue?*

---

1 *The Shack*. Directed by Stuart Hazeldine. Santa Monica, California: Summit Entertainment, 2017. 1:07.05-1:11:00
2 Psalm 139:12

The problem in seeking and finding love is not that we're unworthy, it's that we hide our true selves. Hiding prevents us from experiencing deep and meaningful connections, which prevents us from giving and receiving love. Deep, true love takes vulnerability, nakedness, and letting ourselves be fully known. However, ever since the fall in the garden of Eden,[3] people have been hiding from themselves, from each other, and from God. We don't want to be seen for who we really are.

Many of us hide our true selves for self-protection. We fear what people will think. Our parents unknowingly teach us to do this. They teach us to look a certain way, speak a certain way, and present ourselves in the best light. However, why they teach us to do these things doesn't often get through to us until later in life. Our positive representations of ourselves should be because we love ourselves and others, because we're confident and genuine. It should not be because we're codependent or afraid of what people will think. Neither should it be because we're people-pleasing or think we're responsible for the feelings of others.

We all experience a reality in which we see the world through our own eyes. If we begin to believe we're intimidating, or "too much," or "too quiet," or that something we do or say is wrong or not received well, many of us will self-adjust. We hide. We adapt. We learn what's pleasing to the world around us and quickly create a social version of ourselves that's more acceptable.[4] In many ways, we have become a country of compulsive "white" liars. We have a constant habit of sugar coating our lives and trying to look a certain way in the world, especially on social media, which is not our true self.

Wearing this mask of social appropriateness causes all sorts of problems long-term. Aside from a constant question of worthiness and acceptance: "If they knew the real me, would I still be welcome here?" it also creates an angry, bottled up, and conflict-avoidant society that lashes out in

---

3 Genesis 3
4 Others may choose to embrace their differences and relish in being a misfit, rebelling against society. While this is a different path, it leads to the same place... being rebellious enough to fit in with the other rebels so you can be outside the norm with them. We all have people we adjust for.

unhealthy ways. While many are conflict avoidant when face-to-face, our society actively engages in verbal violence, rejection, and shaming on social media and public news platforms. While some intentionally shout loudly and unapologetically, with a "forget you" attitude if you don't accept their beliefs, others hide in the shadows. Both approaches are just different forms of defensiveness and self-protection. Neither honor Jesus nor the souls around us.

Creating deliberate conflict can also be a mask. Conflict is a form of connection, even if it's unhealthy. When people are isolated and unhealthy, bad attention is better than no attention. Conflict meets a shallow need for connection. By creating a violent verbal conflict, people create chaos and rip at people's hearts from a safe sniper's view away while building camaraderie around murderous hatred.

So many people hate themselves, their lives, the world, and God. Hatred overflows from hearts in destructive ways. The only way people know how to cope with the overwhelming pain of life is to find people at their level to bond with over the pain. There is no greater bond in the world that unites us than finding a common enemy to hate together. But this hateful, verbally-violent conflict is birthed in and breeds evil.

We need Jesus. We need help. We need more love and less hate. Hate may be one of the top-selling social glues on Earth, but the greatest bond in heaven is love. Love might play the long-game, but love always wins in the end.

Seeking and loving and serving God together tears down self-protection and independence, and unites people in healthy interdependence. We go farther together. We were meant to live in community with others.

The longer I live in community, the more I witness healthy hearts being formed in the quiet place. The quiet place is where we sit with the Lord and ask him to seek and know us. It's the place he reveals any wicked way within us,[5] and where we repent and turn to him. It's where we practice the art of vulnerability with the God who created us. The quiet place is where

---

[5] Psalm 139:23-24

we seek true love. It's where we let ourselves be seen and stop trying to hide from the God who sees and knows all things.[6]

God formed your innermost being and knit you together in your mother's womb.[7] He knows everything about you.[8] He knows the number of tears you have cried and the number of hairs on your head.[9] He wants nothing more than to love you and be loved by you. He desires to lavish his love on you.[10] You are his treasured possession.[11]

The way we love others matters, but before we can love others, we must love ourselves. It really matters what we think of ourselves, in the quiet, alone time. Listening to the way the Lord sings over us[12] and spending time with him heals us from the inside out. He takes all our wounds and heals them. He brings light into the dark places. He shapes and molds us to look more like him.

When I say you must love yourself, I am not saying to be a "lover of self."[13] I don't mean being selfish, pleasure-seeking, self-seeking or narcissistic. I don't mean putting your needs above others. Instead, we must be patient with ourselves, be kind to ourselves, and forgive ourselves. We must put our egos aside and humbly accept that we are all broken humans, doing the best we know to do.

For generations, leaders have talked about loving our neighbor and how to love others, but we have left out how to love ourselves.

Over and over, the Bible repeats the greatest commandment, You shall love your neighbor (or the stranger, or your enemy) *as yourself.*[14]

---

6 Job 34:21; Proverbs 5:21
7 Psalm 139:13
8 Psalm 139
9 Matthew 10:29-31
10 1 John 3:1
11 Exodus 19:5
12 Zephaniah 3:17
13 2 Timothy 3:2
14 Leviticus 19:18 and 19:34; Matthew 19:19 and 22:39; Romans 13:9; Galatians 5:14; James 2:8; and many other places.

Loving ourselves and loving others is so connected; it's impossible to holistically speak about one without the other.

We need balance to equally embrace the two sides of this same coin. When we only speak about loving ourselves, we can become lovers of self: selfishly focusing on our independent gain, unconcerned about who we hurt or avoid in the process. If we talk only about loving others, we can become codependent and unhealthy, slowly erasing ourselves as we give into the needs of everyone else. We must love others as we love ourselves. We must love ourselves as we love others.

To love yourself is to be patient and kind with yourself. It means to appreciate the skills and talents you have and the way you were uniquely created. It avoids wishing you could trade your strength or weakness for that of others. It means you like and appreciate you. To love yourself means you don't put yourself down, or beat yourself up, internally, or to others. To love yourself means you're not too proud, thinking you're better than everyone else, but you're humble and keep yourself in check. You're honest about your success and you don't exaggerate, internally to yourself, or outwardly to others. It means you celebrate your victories, especially the ones only you and God know about. It also means you allow yourself be celebrated by others. To love yourself is to allow yourself to be flexible to the world and people around you. It's to enjoy surprises and not demand things go your way all the time. To love yourself is to recognize your limits and pray and ask for help. It means you know you are not the god of your own universe; you know your place and role in the world and pursue it with reckless abandon.

To love yourself is to care for yourself mentally, emotionally, physically, and spiritually. It means to eat well, to keep your body healthy, and to care for this temple[15] God gave you. To enjoy things in moderation and to indulge every so often and not shame yourself for it. It means you listen to your body and what it needs, but with self-control. You don't always give into what it craves, you use wisdom. It means you don't avoid help or

---

[15] "Or do you not know that your body is a temple of the Holy Spirit within you, whom you have from God? You are not your own, for you were bought with a price. So glorify God in your body." 1 Corinthians 6:19-20

therapy when needed. It means you embrace joy and laughter and tears. It means you are honest about your feelings. It means you don't give up on yourself, and you're willing to repeat something even after you failed the first time, because you have faith in yourself. It means you don't resent yourself or regret your past. To love yourself means you recognize you did the best you could at the time and are grateful for the things you learned in hindsight. It means you embrace your mistakes and forgive yourself. It means you appreciate yourself, your tender heart, your rational mind, and your beautiful body. *To love yourself is to see yourself as beautiful.*

With a love that always protects, loving yourself means you cause yourself no intentional harm: not by self-wounding, and not by returning to the things or people who harm you. It means to care for yourself, to consider yourself and your feelings to be equally valuable as others, not more important, not less important. It means to have good boundaries, to speak with authority, not passively or aggressively, but with confidence in where you stand and why. With a love that always trusts and hopes, it means you allow yourself to dream and believe in yourself. Holding these two things in tension means you also don't give up when something harms you. Instead of being a victim or running away from problems, you honestly assess if you're willing to fight for it, and discern when it's worth the effort and when it's time to let go of the haters.

To love yourself means to know yourself, to not avoid any part of your heart or mind that disgusts or scares you. It means you reflect on your experiences, wants, needs, hopes, and failures with honesty, and through the truth that God loves you. It's not to look at yourself with shame or guilt or unworthiness, but to fully embrace, accept, and admire yourself and spur yourself on to grow. It means to be your own best friend, who calls you on your crap. To love yourself is to demand constant growth and not let pain or fear hold you back.

The strength that comes from loving yourself, will make you magnetic. In loving yourself, you naturally love others and lift them up with your positive outlook and encouraging words. That kind of love is contagious. In order to love others as you love yourself, you encourage and walk alongside them while they do the same kind of inner work. You don't do it for them, you do it with them. You hold them accountable, you celebrate their success. You enjoy and appreciate how they're different from you. To love others is to aim to love people as God loves us, with 1 Corinthians 13 love: "Love is patient and kind; love does not envy or boast; it is not arrogant or rude. It does not insist on its own way; it is not irritable or resentful; it does not rejoice at wrongdoing, but rejoices with the truth. Love bears all things, believes all things, hopes all things, endures all things. Love never ends."[16]

For us to love like that takes intention. It takes all you have. You can't stumble into loving like that. I actually don't believe you can do it alone. I think the reason the commandments are in the order they are, with loving God being first, is because loving God is required to successfully do the other. Even with God's aid, we are imperfect. It is impossible to love perfectly all the time, but this should be our prayer and aim. What we do matters. How we act matters.

Just because God says we were worthy of his love before we were born, before we were able to respond and love him in return, doesn't mean our efforts to love him are meaningless. Just because we can gain salvation without works, doesn't mean our works don't matter in the relationship. Our love and loyalty and belief in God without action is dead.[17]

Our intentional pursuit of him is, in fact, worth more than we can imagine.

In 1998, Mike Bickle gave a mini-sermon series on wholehearted love for the Lord, which he referred to as spiritual violence:
> "Jesus gives the principle of wholeheartedness, the principle of spiritual violence, this radical pursuit, this refusing to be denied. The refusing to come up with anything less than God's best for our lives is spiritual violence....he says, [in Matthew 11:12] 'from the days of John the Baptist until now the kingdom of heaven suffers, (put the word it permits, honors, or allows, or rewards) spiritual violence'....spiritually-violent lovers of God

[16] 1 Corinthians 13:4-8
[17] James 2:17

will seize and take things by force that would have been withheld from them if they would have been passive."[18]
Mike goes on to explain how Jesus is telling the crowd the kingdom of heaven has been crashing in on them with violent force. Jesus is saying God has been pursuing them passionately and zealously. He says those who respond to this with spiritual violence, with as much energy and enthusiasm as they can muster, will seize it. He says we should not just pursue God with sincerity, but with wholehearted, violent love. He says many mistake their passive effort for wholeheartedness.[19]

A passive pursuit of a relationship will leave you without one. Those who pursue God passionately, will be able to grasp him and his way of love. The kingdom of God, his reality, is not out of reach for those who seek it,[20] but it is out of reach for those who spend their time pursuing everything else.

Pause and imagine this.

A young child stands before an old, heavy door. It is large and ancient, the height of three men. It's beautifully intricate. It's carved with symbols and inlaid with precious metals and gemstones. The child is fascinated by what's behind the door. The door looks like it could be an entryway to another world. It's breathtaking. Looking at it sparks wonder and curiosity. Whatever this locked door guards must be invaluable.

The Father hands this child the large, golden key, custom made for this lock, for this door. The key has weight to it. It's unique and just as stunning as the door. The child puts the one-of-a-kind key in the beautiful golden lock and tries to turn the key. It doesn't budge. The child looks at Dad, "It won't move."

"Push harder," Dad says with compassion and a smile. He's so proud and excited for his child to open the door and explore the mysterious world on the other side.

---

18 Mike Bickle, "Forerunners with Holy Violent Love Part 1," 6:18, The Mike Bickle Library, posted November 7, 1998, https://mikebickle.org/watch/mb_2353
19 Ibid., 44:26
20 Matthew 7:7-8

The child looks back at the lock and tries again, now with two hands. It barely moves.

"You can do it," Dad says. "Don't give up."

The child focuses and thinks, "If it takes all my body weight, whatever is behind this door is worth it." When the child is so intently focused on getting the key to move, maybe with a foot on the door, straining with all his body weight, Dad's watchful eye is forgotten. Suddenly, Dad's hand seems to come from nowhere. Dad's strong hand, alongside the child's fingers, turns the key in an instant.

God can be like that.

Giving 100 percent of our effort might only put in 2 percent of the strength needed to unlock spiritual doors, but God will only put in 98 percent because he requires we give it our all in partnership with him. He wants a partnership. He wants to do things with us. Only together, will Dad open the door. He doesn't open doors passively. He opens doors with us when we show with our actions we really do want it opened. Most of the time, that action is a state of heart. It is prayer: asking, seeking, knocking. It's not hard, but it does take effort. It takes focus and intentional, wholehearted pursuit.

When we're looking for it, we find God's love is intense and strong and powerful. God's love is so commanding and disarming at times, it can feel violent to us. When we invite him into our whole heart, he will disrupt our lives. As we hand over ourselves to be transformed, he helps us clean out all the clutter and boxes and dust from our past that is blocking that gorgeous door to wholehearted love. Those boxes don't make you unworthy of opening the door, but they are in the way.

Working side by side, God helps us clean out all the things that stand in the way of accessing spiritual doors. Do this long enough, and you'll wonder what boxes you moved, and which ones he moved. You'll wonder where you begin and where he ends, and then, someday, it no longer matters. The whole point is that the process brings you together. Every box you move

Worthy of Love || 83

together brings you closer to God's love. His love isn't just behind the door, it's within reach, now.

Our wholehearted pursuit of God's love will lead us to love as he loves, with spiritual violence. Him for us, us for him. Him through us for others, him through others for us. His love runs through us, is in us, and is resting upon us when we enter into wholeheartedness. To be wholehearted means to overturn and overthrow every other god we rely upon.

Selfishness must go.
Self-protection must go.
Passivity must go.
Everything must go.

I love how Mike defines wholeheartedness.
> "It is violent to enter into wholeheartedness...it is disruptive. It's costly. It's confusing and perplexing to people with unrenewed minds like us. It's disruptive. It's painful. We're unsure; we don't know. It's discombobulating. We don't know the issues yet. And yet the Lord says, go on the journey and it will disrupt everything. There's no such thing as a clean birth. It will be painful. It will be bloody, it will be disruptive, perplexing. It's called by the uncreated God, violence. It's not called 'stumble into it.' You can stumble into the grace of God, into the kingdom of God and be forgiven, but You can't stumble into wholeheartedness."[21]

In order to be loved so intensely and love in return that intensely, there must be trust. We must trust and have faith in how good he is. We must know he is the one who demands our best. He is relentless in his pursuit of us, and yet, he is kind and will never cross a boundary without consent. This God is always standing at the door and knocking.[22] He will never enter without you opening up to him. When you open the door to him, he knocks on another. He is ever asking to be invited in, to commune with you on a deeper level.

21 Bickle, "Forerunners with Holy Violent Love Part 1," 30:32.
22 Revelation 3:20

God is not abusive. He is not rude. He is not pushy. He does not manipulate. We can't even comprehend God's perfect, zealous, meek love. Only in building a relationship with him can we come to recognize this God who is humble and lovely and good and violently jealous for all of our attention. He desires all our heart, all our thoughts, all our strength.

Mike's words are true. Getting closer to God is disruptive. It's costly. Sometimes it's painful. Sometimes I hear him say something and I doubt. I'm unsure. When I resist most, it's probably him, telling me to "pick up my cross"[23] and die to the desires of my selfish ego to serve, love, and humble myself before God and others. It requires an interior, spiritual violence to remove all the boxes that stand in the way of pursuing the things of God with wholeheartedness.

This returns me to loving others. Consider marriage. You can be sincere in a relationship before marriage. You can pursue someone and see them regularly. But when you live with someone and make a covenant to stay together until death, it will take work. Relationships are not always easy. To pursue your spouse wholeheartedly means doing things you don't want to do. It means compromise. It means putting them and their needs before your own sometimes. It requires picking up your cross and dying to the desires of your selfish ego to serve, love, and humble yourself before your spouse. Many relationships end because someone approaches a battle and says to themselves, "I won't die on that hill." They walk away. They would rather kill the relationship than sacrifice their pride and die to their own wants and needs for the benefit of their spouse.

Everything you experience in this world—your relationships, your work, the media, even your church—will be used to violently pull you away from the Lord. Everywhere you turn, it is easy to be offended.

Everywhere you turn, it is easy to judge others and be inflamed with self-righteousness and pride. If you do not intentionally pursue God, you will get off course and start pursuing something else.

---

[23] "If anyone would come after me, let him deny himself and take up his cross daily and follow me." Luke 9:23

This is a world of tug-of-war.
If you don't hold on to Jesus, you will get pulled into the mud.
You'll also get pulled into the mud if you're alone. You need a team.

Jesus said, "Just as I have loved you, you also are to love one another."[24] Since he loves every one of us with a jealous love, we must also love each other with passionate pursuit. We must spur each other along in love, always actively pursuing love for the Lord, ourselves, and each other. We need to work together in unity.

In the book of James, he regards, "You shall love your neighbor as yourself" as the "royal law."[25] Since we are the bride in this epic love story, preparing ourselves to meet Jesus, our bridegroom, then we are on a life-long transformational journey to make ourselves ready to reign as royalty alongside him.[26] I don't just mean in heaven, in the afterlife. I mean now, today. Since God wants partners, we need to be transformed internally, into a partner ready to rule alongside him. He doesn't want to rule over us, so much as he wants us to rule with him.

If the kingdom of heaven is here, now, let's embrace our role as heirs and ambassadors in a divine kingdom of love, here and now. You may not have seen the church do this, but it is possible to walk with strength and confidence in our authority and identity as a chosen, loved, son or daughter of the King. It is also possible to encourage, edify, and raise up those around you to walk in that same God-given identity.

Jesus deserves a bride that wants to spend time with him, who loves him and loves his people the way he loved us, with active servant-leadership. Lukewarm commitment because of religious obligation is not enough for the King of Creation. The One who could have anything, chose us. His actions proclaimed we were worthy of a love as strong as death. He also, is worthy of such love.

---

24 John 13:34
25 James 2:8
26 2 Timothy 2:12

Return to Love

Our wounds and failures do not make us unworthy. We are wounded and he was wounded for us. In this, God lowered himself to be equal to us. He deemed us worthy and chose us before we were born. We must rise to meet him in passionate desire.

To reign alongside Jesus today, and in the future, he wants our active, wholehearted love. Our wholehearted love is the only thing we can offer him. It's the only thing the Creator of the universe does not already have. He owns everything.[27] The only thing he does not have is our love, our praise, our thanks.

If you grew up in some kind of Christian background, you might have heard a lot about needing to get to know God. You might have been taught you should read your bible or pray or go to church on Sundays to learn about him. But when Jesus talks about the way to live, he speaks of his return and says the way is narrow. He says people will come to him at the end, expecting to reside with him, and he will say to many, "I never knew you, depart from me."[28] That's a terrifying scripture. He does not say, "Depart from here, you do not know me;" he refuses entry to those who did not let themselves be known. It's easy to read about God and learn about him, to claim you know him. It is much harder to crack open the depths of our heart, mind, and soul to the God of the universe and be fully known. The safest place to be fully known and fully loved is in God's good, holy, perfect presence.

Anyone who has fallen in love knows building a healthy relationship takes communication—both ways. We must get to know each other, spend time with each other, learn to trust and love each other. Over time, we get to know each other's quirks and preferences. We move towards commitment, where we promise to walk through life together. We promise to have eyes only for each other. You trust him or her with your whole heart and put all your eggs in one basket.

In our relationship with God, it's the same. It means giving him your all. It means learning to love and trust him by walking through life with him. It

---
27 Psalm 50:12
28 Matthew 7:24

means not worshiping any another God. It means being weak, vulnerable, and naked in his presence. Divine love has no walls, no masks.

Tearing down the masks starts at home. It starts alone, in the secret place, with only God as your witness. If you can't be authentic and honest with yourself and with God, you won't be able to be vulnerable with others either. You have to love yourself in order to love others.

We must admit and see that while there is darkness within us, we are also lovely.[29] We must accept and love ourselves, as we are. If we are always striving to be enough, we will never be satisfied. If we focus on the darkness, we will find ourselves trapped in the midst of it, but if we call out to the Lord of light,[30] the darkness will flee.[31] The ugly cycle of striving to be enough will keep someone trapped until they invite God to heal and transform him or her from the inside out.

When we choose to love God with all we have, he will start to clean out the darkness and revive the parts of us that are dead. In the Old Testament, there is a story where God asks his friend if a valley full of dead bones can live again.[32] Ezekiel looks at the valley and says, "Lord, you are the only one who knows if that's possible." God breathes on them and resurrects them back to life. To these resurrected bodies, God even promises to fulfill the promises he made while they were still alive.

God can do that. He can bring things back to life to fulfill his promises. He wants to breathe on every dead part of our hearts and bring us back to a life of love. Like me, you might not even know the part of your heart that is hard, wounded, or bleeding. Often what he wants to remove or heal is a surprise to us. Nothing is impossible for him.[33] To us, the lackluster state of our heart is normal, but God can give us *a new normal.*

---

29 Song of Solomon 1:5
30 John 1:5
31 John 1:9
32 Ezekiel 37
33 Matthew 19:26

Return to Love

It's not always easy when God asks us to give things up to make space for more love in our hearts. He searches our hearts and knows all things.[34] He tests the hearts of men and women.[35] He doesn't always ask us to give up everything forever, but he is willing to test us.

One of the most controversial stories in the Bible might be God testing Abraham. After years of waiting for the promised child, Isaac, God tells Abraham to kill him. He tells Abraham to sacrifice Isaac as a burnt offering.

Before we continue, I have to note that, historically, it was common for ancient people to sacrifice their children to their gods. When Abraham hears this, he is hearing something that is common in his day to other religions. While it's appalling to us today, it wouldn't have been that far outside of the cultural worldview of the time.

Abraham rises early in the morning and goes out to do as he is told. Abraham travels for three days, and on the way, Isaac asks him where the animal is for the sacrificial offering. Abraham prophetically replies, "God will provide."[36]

On the third day, Abraham prepares everything for the sacrifice. Just as he's about to obey the command of the Lord and kill his son, the Lord stops him, "Do not lay your hand on the boy or do anything to him, for now I know you fear God, seeing you have not withheld your son, your only son from me."[37]

God tested Abraham's heart.

This story is clearly a foreshadowing of Jesus. God has chosen Abraham to be the father of Israel. Israel is the nation that will be beloved of the Lord. The future Messiah, God's son, will come through Abraham's bloodline. Abraham is a man who loves the Lord so much he's willing to give God his only son. Two thousand years later, God loved the world so much he gave us

---

34 Psalm 139:1; Psalm 139:23
35 Jeremiah 17:10; Proverbs 17:3
36 Genesis 22:8
37 Genesis 22:12

his only son to die for both Israel and us. It's interesting that the Lord tests Abraham to see if he would be willing to do the same for God.

Maybe this God who sees into the hearts of man, knew that Abraham loved his son so much, he would be tempted to do anything for him. Maybe he would have been tempted to sin and disobey the Lord on behalf of his son, in a desire to please or protect his son over the will of the Lord. Through passing this test, Abraham proved to God and (maybe more importantly) to himself, that God had first place in his heart. He proved his allegiance was to follow the Lord, no matter the loss in his own life. This test showed Abraham that he loved God even more than he loved his promised son. Abraham proved through his action that he would put God first, above all else.

The emotional turmoil and grief Abraham must have gone through on the three day journey and in the actual act of binding Isaac, must have been tremendous. He probably bonded with his son and loved him more than ever those last three days, determined to cherish every moment, in case it was the last. He also, undoubtedly, prayed constantly that the Lord would change his mind. I'm sure his prayer was similar to Jesus before the cross: "Father, if you are willing, remove this cup from me. Nevertheless, not my will, but yours, be done."[38]

However, Abraham also believed in God's promise, "Through Isaac shall your offspring be named."[39] Therefore, "He considered that God was able even to raise him from the dead."[40] He believed his friend could bring his son back to life. He had enough faith to obey and trust. He had enough faith to ignore his physical perspective and look from a heavenly perspective.

He trusted the Lord and knew his character. He knew God was faithful to his promises, because he had walked through a twenty-five year journey waiting for a miracle baby. He had experience and relational equity with the Lord. They were friends. So while Abraham didn't fully understand

---

38 Luke 22:42
39 Hebrews 11:18
40 Hebrews 11:19

the reason his friend was making this request, he knew his friend could be trusted.

That's wholehearted love.
That's spiritual violence.

God loves you as you are. He says you are worthy. But like all of us who want the very best for the ones we love, he also wants us to pursue and ask and reach for our best. Our best includes an intimate, wholehearted relationship with him, where he is involved in every piece of our lives.

Mike Bickle said, "God reserves the fullest measure of his blessing for those who are spiritually violent or are wholehearted in their pursuit of God.... [Spiritual violence/Wholeheartedness] is an invitation to live a lifestyle where you will not settle for anything than God's best."[41]

When we wholeheartedly pursue God,
we gain more of him and more of his blessing.
When we go all in, we seek and find his best.
His best, is our best.

Not only was Abraham blessed, but God promised, through Abraham, the whole world would be blessed.[42] Abraham did not settle for contentment and comfort. He was willing to die to his own desires and humble himself before his friend to say, "Your will, not mine." He obeyed God wholeheartedly. *He knew God's way was better than his way, even if he didn't understand.*

Quick pause, so I can be clear.

I'm not saying God will ask you to do something like that in order to pursue him. I'm positive, in fact, that he will not ask you to sacrifice your child, because Jesus came and died for you. Don't get it twisted. Let's all be thankful many things have changed in the thousands of years since Abraham.

---

41 Bickle, "Forerunners with Holy Violent Love Part 1," 36:28.
42 Genesis 22:18

Worthy of Love || 91

I am saying, sometimes, God asks us to trust him with our most precious dreams, and hand them over to be fulfilled in his way and his timing. Handing it over may be painful, but we must trust. What looks bad to us might actually be good in a little while, and what looks good to us might actually be detrimental to us in the long run. God goes ahead of us and knows the outcome.

There is an old proverb about a farmer who, no matter what happens to him, does not attribute good or bad luck to the situation. Instead, he always answers, "We'll see." I see a similar proverb in the story of Abraham's great-grandson, Joseph.[43]

Joseph was his father's favorite. He was given a beautiful robe by his father. He had two dreams that all his family bowed down to him. Looks good, but we'll see.

His favor made his brothers hate him. They wanted to kill him, but decided it was better for them if they got rid of him and made a little money. So they sold him into slavery. Looks bad, but we'll see.

Joseph was sold by the slave traders in Egypt to one of Pharaoh's officials. He rose up and up in responsibility. His master trusted him and relied on him. He became very successful and grew to be a handsome man. Looks good, but we'll see.

The official's wife sexually harassed Joseph and pressured him to sleep with her. Joseph did the right thing and ran away from her, but she told her husband that he tried to come on to her because she wanted to punish him for not giving in to her. The official was furious and threw Joseph in prison. Looks bad, but we'll see.

Joseph's good character gained him favor in the prison as well. The prison warden placed him in charge of other prisoners. One day, two of Pharaoh's officials were sent to prison and Joseph attended to them. They had disturbing dreams one night, and Joseph interpreted their dreams

---
43 Genesis 37-50

accurately. He asks one, "When you are restored, please remember me, because I don't deserve to be in this place." Looks good, but we'll see.

The official was restored, as Joseph predicted, but he forgot about Joseph. Looks bad, but we'll see.

Years later, Pharaoh has two dreams and is disturbed by them. He desires an interpretation. The official remembers Joseph and tells Pharaoh about him. Pharaoh calls Joseph out of prison and Joseph correctly interprets the dreams, telling him God is warning him that famine is coming. He tells Pharaoh how to prepare for the famine so all of Egypt and the surrounding area can be saved. Pharaoh is so pleased with his wisdom that he places Joseph in charge of all of Egypt, only one step below the throne. Joseph works to execute his proposed plan. After seven years of successful preparation, famine begins and he successfully saves all of Egypt and the surrounding areas. This includes Joseph's family. His brothers arrive, asking to purchase food, and after they are reconciled, the whole family moves to be close to Joseph so they can survive the famine as well. Looks good, but we'll see....

Reflecting, Joseph could have been upset at God for all the seemingly bad things that happened to him, but he continued to walk with the Lord. He listened and was close enough to the Lord that he could hear the interpretation of dreams. The whole story began with him having two dreams, and knowing what they meant, that his whole family would eventually bow down to him. Later, when Pharaoh has two dreams, Joseph says, "The doubling of Pharaoh's dream means that the thing is fixed by God, and God will shortly bring it about."[44]

Joseph lived a rollercoaster. He could have doubted. He could have lost faith. In Psalms, it says the word of the Lord tested him until it came to pass.[45] He would have wrestled, like any man, but he held onto those dreams with enough faith that he could turn to Pharaoh and say with confidence, a double dream given to you by God is fixed and it will come to pass, even though he had not yet seen his dreams come to pass.

44 Genesis 41:32
45 Psalm 105:19

Worthy of Love

At the end of the story, Joseph says to his brothers, "You intended to harm me, but God intended it for good to accomplish what is now being done, the saving of many lives."[46] He wrested to keep his faith and trust in the Lord throughout his journey. But, the end result was worth the journey of testing. In hindsight, all the ups and downs made sense to him and he was able to reassure others that their evil actions did not hinder God's good and perfect will.

The Lord tells us to remember his great works and the way he leads us. He says to remember how he humbles us and tests us to know what is in our hearts and whether or not we'll obey him.[47] Remembering must be important. We are quick to forget blessings that come easily, but we remember the pain and hard seasons that led to a big pay out. When we do things in our own strength, we reap a little reward, but when we partner with the King of the Universe, our little dream evolves into his dream, and we reap more than we could imagine.

Long before we voluntarily partner with him, whether we admit it or not, **we are completely dependent on the God who is in control of everything we cannot control.**

Jesus was pointing out our dependency upon him when he taught "whoever feeds on me, he also will live because of me. This is the bread that came down from heaven...whoever feeds on this bread will live forever."[48]

Many of the disciples stopped following Jesus when he said this. So, he asked his inner circle, "Do you want to go away as well?"

One of them answered, "Where else would we go? You have the words of eternal life, and we have believed, and have come to know, that you are the Holy One of God."[49]

I ask that same thing to the Lord, often.

---

46 Genesis 50:20
47 Deuteronomy 8:2
48 John 6:57-58
49 Luke 6:66-69

Return to Love

At some point along the journey of believing in this great and marvelous God, you begin to trust the Lord. He really does ask people to be missionaries in dangerous places. He really does ask some to put their lives on the line for him. He really does ask all of us some version of the question he asked Abraham, "Do you love me more than the thing you love most in life?" And when you finally realize he's all-powerful and asks you to do counter-cultural, seemingly crazy things, you're already all in. You've fallen in love and it's too late to go back to life as it was before knowing him. Even if you could, you wouldn't want to, because he's worth it all.

When God asks you to be patient and wait for his best and not settle for instant gratification...
When God asks you to die to your selfishness and both forgive and apologize to someone...
When God asks if you're willing to speak even if people will hate you[50] for what you say...
You'll answer with me, "Of course, where else would I go?"

From this perspective, I understand Abraham. He was sold-out; he was all in. Abraham had bet everything on the Lord, everything on what God said, everything on who God is and was and will be. Abraham believed and trusted in God, and it was counted to him as righteousness.[51] It wasn't because he was perfect; we know Abraham wasn't perfect. It was Abraham's trust and confidence in the Lord, his fidelity and loyalty, his faith, that made him righteous in God's eyes. This is the kind of faith that makes us pray, "Your will, Lord; not mine. Do whatever it takes to let me love you with all my heart, mind, and strength."

That might be a dangerous prayer, but it's worth it.

I mentioned to you that when I arrived in Kansas City for the internship, I wanted to be all in, but I didn't know how. That u-turn prayer in June 2019 brought more healing to me than any other. I said something like, "I'm sorry, Lord. I didn't know my heart was holding that much pain. Your will

---

50 Matthew 24:9-13
51 James 2:23; Genesis 15:6

be done, not mine. I trust you have a plan and you know what you're doing. If that's why you brought me here, to heal and soften my heart and prepare me for what's next, I'll do it. Let's get started."

In the short term, that prayer was painful. It required me to let go of what I wanted and what I thought was best for me. It required me to let go of self-protection and allow myself to be vulnerable. It required that I trust him more than I trusted my own understanding. It meant trusting the Great Physician to expertly remove the woundedness around my heart, perform surgery like only he could, let myself be weak and vulnerable, and then rest and recover. Now that I know where it led me, I wouldn't have it any other way.

Months after hearing that word from the Lord, that he wanted me to get married again, I doubted my memory. I was struggling to believe I had heard him correctly. I was at church and a stranger approached me. She said the Lord told her to tell me to look with my spiritual eyes, not with my physical eyes. When I doubted, he sent encouragement. When the winds of testing came, he sent support. He was faithful to keep my faith alive.

It was one of those seasons, where I continued to ask myself, "Where else would I go?" I had to trust that the path I was on would eventually make more sense. I thought to myself and the Lord, "I might as well keep going if you've led me this far." I knew he had orchestrated my move to Kansas City with a scholarship, finances, and a place to live. He had been intentional about leading me there.

In those kinds of seasons, where you can't see or make sense of everything, you must obey his command to remember. I had to remember he had been faithful before, throughout my life. He had fulfilled many of the words he spoke. I had to trust he was about to fulfill many more. I was all in. It was time to stop listening to my rollercoaster of emotions and choose to be grateful for what he had already done. It was time to release my expectations and be patient. It was time to sit and watch the rest of his plan manifest before my eyes in his perfect timing. He taught me how to be completely dependent on him in that season and the one that followed.

All my chips were on God fulfilling his promises and knowing there was absolutely nothing I could do except wait.

I had bet *everything* I had on God.

Shadrach, Meshach, and Abednego also bet everything they had on God. When King Nebuchadnezzar demanded his citizens bow down and worship an idol he created, these three men refused.[52] Being Jews, they lived by the Ten Commandments. This is the first two of the Ten Commandments: "You shall have no other gods before me. You shall not make for yourself a carved image, or any likeness of anything that is in heaven above, or that is in the earth beneath, or that is in the water under the earth. You shall not bow down to them or serve them, for I the Lord your God am a jealous God."[53]

When Nebuchadnezzar found out about their disobedience, he threw them in a fiery furnace. It was so hot that even the mighty men who bound and tossed them inside died from the intense heat. But once inside, Nebuchadnezzar could see not just three men, but also an angel with them, and they came out completely unharmed. No hair was singed, there was not even the smell of fire on their clothes. Because of this miracle, the king and his entire nation recognized the God of Israel.

When Shadrach, Meshach, and Abednego put their lives on the line and chose to go all in, they said to King Nebuchadnezzar, "If we are thrown into the blazing furnace, the God whom we serve is able to save us. He will rescue us from your power, Your Majesty. But even if he doesn't, we want to make it clear to you, Your Majesty, that we will never serve your gods or worship the gold statue you have set up." (NLT)[54]

Talk about a mic drop!

---

52 Daniel 3
53 Exodus 20:3-5
54 Daniel 3:17-18, NLT. Scripture quotations marked (NLT) are taken from the *Holy Bible, New Living Translation*, copyright © 1996, 2004, 2007, 2013 by Tyndale House Foundation. Used by permission of Tyndale House Publishers, Inc., Carol Stream, Illinois 60188. All rights reserved.

When you're all in, those words ring true. I knew God was able to save and preserve me from the fire of testing, but I also knew if he didn't, I must refuse to bow down and worship fear, doubt, or apathy. I knew even if he "took away" the dream I had imagined for my future self, he was still good, and there was a reason for it all. I trusted my friend. I trusted him to transform me while I waited for him to act.

Everything we experience is an invitation to be transformed.

When I thought everything I had was already in the pot, when I thought all my chips were in, God would say, "What about that over there, will you put that in?" And I would. Again and again, he asks for more. "What about that over there that you forgot about, would you give that to me? Will you go all in with me? Will you trust me?"

Over and over and over for the rest of my life, I will say, "Yes, Lord. Where else would I go? I love you, and I know you ask because you are jealous for my whole heart. I will give it to you one piece at a time."

When you receive a vision, dream, or promise from the Lord that might take years to unfold, what do you do? You go bury that pearl, and then you go sell everything you own and buy the field where you buried it.[55] You have to go all in. You have to trust him when you reach the end of yourself, and the end of what you can control.

Life on this planet requires death and resurrection. Every seed must go in the ground and be buried, where only God sees its progress and makes it grow, without any influence of our own. We might water a seed, but even God brings the rain. We do nothing except wait with patience and anticipation for his wondrous work. Only God can make the seed grow. We have to surrender, realize we have no power, and be completely dependent on God.

Going all in will set off all the alarms in your head. It makes you realize you will look like the biggest fool on the planet if God doesn't come through for

---
55 Matthew 13:44

you. And then you realize even that feeling has to go in the pot. Fear has to go. People-pleasing must go. All the things that stand in the way must be handed over, so you can love without hesitation.

To love without restraint is to love like Jesus loves. We must love ourselves and others without restraint. Personal growth and intimacy with God is the only thing that really matters in life because our internal transformation affects everything else. Your external experience cannot outgrow your internal experience. What happens internally, between you and Jesus, in the secret place, is the seed. That seed of love begins to grow vertically at first, towards him, and then horizontally towards others.

While on the outside my life looked messy and wild, even to me, God saw differently. God knew the potential for growth. When he asked, "Do you trust me?" and to hand things over, he was leading me through a process. He was watching over a transformation that would take place from the inside out. He was uprooting darkness in my soul, removing barriers, and tilling the ground for a fruitful and lush next season. He was composting everything I had learned and showing me all the beautiful life that could come out of previous seasons of death and decay. He was breathing life into my dead bones.

In the secret place, he taught me how to love myself, appreciate my messy life, and trust he was able to redeem and repurpose everything I thought was lost. Nothing is lost in his hands; he knows how to repurpose everything for good.[56] He knows how to reframe our experiences in order to teach us how to love ourselves, him, and others more.

All you have to do is ask.

---

56 Romans 8:28

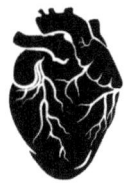

Invitation to Prayer

Lord, would you help me reframe my messy life?
Would you show me how you're working all of this for good?
Would you teach me how to love and forgive myself for the messes I've made? Would you open my eyes to see the perfect process you have planned? Would you breathe life into my dead bones?
Would you perform surgery on my heart?
Show me if there is anything that stands in the way of me loving you more.
Is there anything I put above you that you want from me?
Tell me, Lord. Speak to me. Open my ears to hear you. Test my heart.
Help me get to a place where I'm ready to go all in. I want to be fully known by you. I want to say, "Yes," to you and partner with you to tear down the mindsets and lies and strongholds that stop me from being fully known and embracing your zealous love.
I'm asking for a new normal. I'm asking that you bring me to a place where I pursue you wholeheartedly. I'm asking to stand confidently before you, as my raw, vulnerable, naked, accepted self, without any walls or masks between us. I don't want to hide anymore.
I want to know I am worthy of your passionate, zealous love for me.
You died for me and said I was worthy of love before I was born.
You are worthy of passionate love in return. I choose love and vulnerability over self-protection, but in my own power and in my own strength,
I will not succeed. I need your help, Jesus.
Come teach me how to love myself, you, and others more.
Amen.

Becoming Friends

Ever since I was a little girl I longed to draw near to Jesus. He called to me in dreams and visions. He wooed me in the unhindered imagination of a young child. My mother claims I spent most of my childhood reading books alone in my room. I had dolls and other normal things, but I loved being alone with Jesus: learning, imagining, creating, and reading.

When I entered the prayer room, a piece of my inner child was revived. It was as if I was returning to a safe and familiar place, though I'd never been there before. It was almost natural to return to a life of reading and listening to Jesus and all he had to say. I had studied and practiced contemplative prayer in seminary, silent prayer in which you spend time in God's presence. That was great, this was even better. Now, I had a live band to serenade the Lord day and night and seek him alongside me.

This way of life leads one to being some sort of mystic, whether in the traditional sense, like St. Teresa of Avila, St. John of the Cross, and St. Bernard of Clairvaux, or in the modern, less-traditional and more critically-thinking sort, such as C.S. Lewis. While many people who have been called "mystic" might not appreciate the label, I'm sure they would agree that to be an intimate friend of Jesus does take a special kind of different.

If that's the case, the Biblical prophets were first in line for the "mystic" label. John the Baptist living on locusts and honey in the desert and Ezekiel laying on his side for four hundred and thirty days to bear the sins of Israel and Judah are just two examples of lives dedicated to voluntary sacrifice, prophecy, and passionate pursuit of the Lord. Living that kind of life, set-apart from the culture, makes someone a weird mystic for sure. These men endured the tension of coexisting in both the spiritual and the physical.

We all see the world through our physical eyes: pain, hardship, and all the ways we fall short. To be a friend of the Lord means to conjunctively see the world through his eyes: full of potential, love, and redemptive purpose.

To wholeheartedly live with our eyes open to the physical and spiritual truly takes balance and Divine help. It is impossible to be in the world and not of the world[1] without the Lord's help. If we ask, he will guard us and protect us from evil. Thankfully, we are not the first to live in the tension of being friends with God.

The Old Testament gives us a glimpse into how the prophets managed to wrestle with God and his ways. They wrestled with the evil and suffering in the world and they argued with God as they witnessed life unfold both personally and nationally. My favorite testimony of arguing with God is the prophet Habakkuk. He plainly states a complaint before the Lord, and then sits down and waits to hear God's reply, anticipating correction.[2] I love this because he honors two sides of the story, both physical and spiritual. He is mature enough to be honest with the Lord and humble enough to recognize the limits of his human understanding. He knows he is dust compared to the living, ineffable God and still believes that this very same God wants to know him. He believes God wants to hear his opinion and considers it valuable because of their friendship. Habakkuk displays his human heart before the Lord: honestly resistant and honestly humble. We are blessed to witness his vulnerable wrestle, so we can aspire to be like him.

---

1 John 17
2 Habakkuk 2:1

We should wrestle with our own thoughts and emotions before God and with God. We should contend with him for our perspective while recognizing that he knows and sees more than we do. It is good for our hearts and minds to be open and honest with God. It is good to say, "I don't understand and I don't like what you're doing!" Being honest and vulnerable helps us clarify what's going on within us. Inviting the Holy Spirit into these moments will transform us and help us understand the bigger picture. In his presence, we humble ourselves and admit, "In the midst of all this stress and emotional turmoil, I know you're smarter than me. I know you have our eternal relationship in mind and you are mindful of me and intend to bless me.[3] I know you are with me and never leave me.[4] I trust you have a good and perfect plan to sort everything out.[5] Please help me to be patient and wait for your response."

It's good to humble ourselves and ask, "Who am I to argue with the I AM?"

God is listening and wants to hear your voice, even when you're angry. He knows all things anyway, so you might as well be honest. But while you're honest, be honestly vulnerable and truthful about your limits and weaknesses. Lean in to trust him. You're safe with him. God can handle your human temper tantrums and misunderstandings. Not only is he patient during the time it takes for you to work through them, but he's cheering you on and sorting through it with you.

When you desire to follow God, it requires that you submit to his leadership. When Habakkuk decides, "I'm going to sit down, hear what he has to say, and then pay attention to how my heart responds to his correction," he puts his relationship with God as the primary focus. He didn't argue to get his way. He approached the Lord because the rift in his understanding would have hurt their relationship in the long run. Instead of being offended by God's actions or lack thereof, he approaches the Lord to reconcile and understand his way and his will. He approaches the Lord with the knowledge that God is a good and perfect leader at the forefront of his mind.

---
[3] Psalm 115:12-13
[4] Deuteronomy 31:8
[5] Jeremiah 29:11

When you have to tell a friend they have hurt or offended you and make peace with them, you have to get vulnerable and real. The best way to do this is to trust their good intentions and keep careful watch over your heart to guard against being offended. You choose reconciliation because you do not want the issue to drive a wedge between you. It's also helpful to remember all you've done together and why you chose to be in the relationship in the first place. It's imperative that we do this with the Lord. It's foolish to ignore that we can feel offended by God's ways. We can be offended by God just as easily as we can be by a human friend.

We grow through being in dynamic relationships with God and others. We grow in patience when we have to wait for others to act. We grow in compassion when someone near us suffers an unexpected turn of events. We grow in kindness when the people around us are annoying and frustrating and we bite our tongue and forgive. We don't grow in faith, trust, or intimacy by flipping a switch. We grow in character and integrity over time.

In all of these circumstances, it's our heart posture that dictates our potential for growth. We get to choose:
Disconnection or Connection
Anger or Patience
Despair or Hope
Hatred or Love

And when we don't have the strength to posture our hearts correctly and act in love, God tells us to ask for help. When we ask, he provides. God's strength is revealed in our weak moments.[6] I can't tell you how many times a simple prayer has shifted my day. Instead of stressing about being late, or growing irritable and impatient with a long line, I shift my focus to prayer. My little cry for help might sound something like this: "Lord, I ask you to be in charge of my time and schedule today. I pray that instead of being late, my next appointment will be timed perfectly for each other's needs. Give me patience and confidence in your divine timing. I ask you to bless the people around me and do the same for them. Please provide supernatural

---

6 2 Corinthians 12:9

peace for that crying baby and its mama...." When you do this, both your heart posture and the atmosphere around you will shift.

Why perpetuate negativity? Jesus asks us, "Which of you by being anxious can add a single hour to his span of life?"[7] Why worry about tomorrow? Why worry about being late or worry about a long line? We might as well spend our time praying and blessing the people around us.

Prayer is the only thing that will shift both our hearts and the atmosphere.

With a little prayer to surrender, we hand over the expectations we had for our day and our schedule. With a quick shift in perspective, we appreciate the pause and enjoy the experience of being present in the moment. It allows us to be present to life occurring around us. With this attitude, we connect with gratitude. With this perspective, we find joy in the little things.

To be a friend of God, you must spend time with him. The best time, is all the time. When you consistently and continually speak to him about everything, you invite him into every moment. He's always with you, but you may not be aware of his abiding presence. Talking to him like a friend will open your ears to listen like a friend. If you

live like this, he'll be involved in all you do. Instead of worrying about little things like what to gift your Mom for her birthday, you'll ask, "What should I get Mom for her birthday?" And then, when you're at the store, you notice something you wouldn't have thought of getting before. He intervenes. He nudges. He shows up in the details. God helps when you ask. He will guide you in the little and the big things.

Praying without ceasing is a way of life.[8]

Since I was young, I understood God was my friend. I knew he listened and <u>wanted to know me</u> because he loved me. I figured if Jesus loved me enough

---

7 Luke 12:25
8 1 Thessalonians 5:17

to die for me, then he must like me. He was my constant and closest friend. I never felt alone, because I was always praying. God was always near. He cared about everything, had the best advice, and gave me peace when I was stressed. He was the best listener and always brought comfort and guidance.

However, at some point in time, I somehow felt like I had to prove myself to him and earn his love. In moving from childhood to adulthood, I lost my innocent perspective of the Lord. Instead of awe and wonder of his capacity for love and confidence that he genuinely liked me and wanted to be near me, I felt distant from him.

Even though my mind knew the truth, that he wanted to be close, there seemed to be a barrier or glass wall in the way. In my experience, if there was a wall up between someone and myself, I must have done something wrong. So when I felt the lack of connection, I was sure I caused it, but I didn't know how to fix it.

Among the many things I used to try to tear down the wall, one was destructive and one was the antidote. Focusing on the negative and the problem was destructive. Focusing on God and all that is good was the antidote. Fixating on my self-improvement and doing everything I could to do better, love better, and achieve more was helpful, but it wasn't enough. I still felt unfulfilled. While fixating on myself, I was desperate for answers and looking for him in everything, but I wasn't letting him fill me. The antidote to both the wall and trying to figure out what was wrong, was to stop looking at myself or my circumstances and focus on him. Just like a lover or friend, if I felt disconnected from him, I just needed to spend time with him. Looking to God and all the good things that come from him was the key to connection.

Paul writes to the Philippians and tells them to meditate on what is true, honorable, good, just, pure, lovely, commendable, excellent, and worthy of praise.[9] If we focus on the God who is the source of all these things, we will become what we behold. We will be transformed into his likeness.

---

9 Philippians 4:8

Becoming Friends || 107

He's so beautiful. This God with eyes of fire[10] looks into our soul and burns away all the darkness. There is no other who loves you so purely and deeply. There is no one better to pour your love upon. There is no one better to spend your time with. It's mind-blowing how much he loves us and that he wants to simply be with us.

Jesus' prayer to be with us is recorded in John 17. "Father, I desire that they also, whom you have given to me, may be with me where I am, to see my glory that you have given me because you loved me before the foundation of the world."[11] He asks that we would become one with him and with each other. "I in them and you in me, that they may become perfectly one, so that the world may know that you sent me and loved them even as you loved me."[12] This is proof that the Lord wants to be with you.

Jesus wants intimacy and connection, i.e. communion. Communion is "sharing or exchanging intimate thoughts and feelings, especially when the exchange is on a mental or spiritual level."[13] You can experience genuine communion in a real, intimate relationship with a personal God. When we accept that we are loved and accepted, and invited to be in communion with Jesus; every moment, every second, of every day, just as we are, we enter a new normal.

It's similar to falling in love with your spouse. All of a sudden, the world is brighter, there is a skip in your step, and a knowing smile on your lips. Your life circumstances and habits didn't change, but something special was added into your heart and it changes everything. When you know someone loves you, you feel accepted and wanted. You don't need to look a certain way or put on an act. You are invited to be yourself.

When we know we are accepted and wanted, we are no longer afraid of being rejected. The God who knows everything, even the deepest secrets of your heart that you still have yet to discover, will not reject you. He was

---

10 Revelation 2:18
11 John 17:24
12 John 17:23
13 *Google's English Dictionary by Oxford Languages*, s.v. "communion," accessed May 26, 2021, https://www.google.com/search?q=Communion.

with you, even when you did the thing you thought made you unworthy of his love. Therefore, there is no reason to hide anything, deny anything, or act a certain way for God or towards God.

I am not saying it's acceptable to be disrespectful or irreverent. Peter advises us, "live as people who are free, not using your freedom as a cover-up for evil, but living as servants of God."[14] In other words, don't use the cross as an excuse to get away with whatever sin or evil you want. That is mocking God. People who claim to be Christian might do that, but wholehearted followers of Jesus do not.

Be honest with the Lord, and with yourself, about the struggle to live in both worlds. It is an unavoidable struggle if you want to live authentically in both a spiritual and physical reality. There is no reason to pretend or be fake about your experience in front of an all-knowing God. You can talk to him like you're talking to a friend. You can argue and make a case. You can cry and let out all those bottled-up emotions. Tell him how people and coworkers and your family are treating you and how you know he says to love them, but how you'd really rather not. You can be honest. It's ok to say, "Sometimes I want you more than anything, Lord, and sometimes believing in you is counterintuitive." He will listen. In fact, I'm sure he'd prefer honesty.

Even when we aim to be genuine and truthful, habits and the way we were raised can sneak up and trick us. Even when it's sincere or natural to act a certain way, it might not be right and good. For example, I was well trained by my Christian upbringing to say, "Your will be done" to God. I was taught to surrender and believe his way was better than mine. This is true, and I will always pray this prayer. But, all things at their extreme are unhelpful, including over-righteousness.[15]

For a season, I was praying, "Your will be done" as a daily breath prayer. Both then and now, I sincerely desire to surrender my future to the Lord. I trust he knows what's best for me and I know my heart can lead me astray.

---

14 1 Peter 2:16
15 Ecclesiastes 7:16-18

But, I didn't know how much praying this would wear me down. Over time, my drastic surrender made me limp. I lost my boldness, my edge, my confidence. I lost my drive and my every desire. I found myself believing my dreams, hopes, and desires were meaningless. I wasn't partnering with God's will to be done on earth, as I should. I was asking him to empty me out in an unhealthy way. I was assuming he didn't care about what I wanted. I was forgetting that he was the very one who created me and placed desires in my heart.[16] This very good and true and wonderful prayer was twisted to cause harm. I was erasing myself and my dreams to replace them with what I was taught to be the epitome of holiness.

When we pray for the Lord's will to be done in a specific thing, to reveal a path, the Lord will provide hope and direction. When we pray for his will to be done on Earth as it is in Heaven,[17] we're asking for his kingdom's reality to manifest itself down here. This prayer of surrender should not have caused me to compare my imperfect will with his perfect will in a way that erased my will or dreams, but I was surrounded by people who were placing righteousness over relationship and they were rubbing off on me. I was losing myself and I needed to be reminded that he gave me a will for a reason.

Soon, I started hearing the Lord ask me what I wanted. At first, I replied, "I want whatever you want, Lord." He knew I was in an unhealthy mindset, and he wasn't going to let me keep going down that path. No good man wants a spineless, passionless, detached woman. No good friend always wants to pick where you eat dinner. A good friend wants to know what you want. They like and respect and desire your opinions and your voice.

One day, God replied to me, "I want what you want, Alena. What do you want?" I was in a catch-22. At this point, I had forgotten what I wanted. I had to start at the very bottom and pick a new mountain to climb. "Help, Lord. I want to know what I want. Show me my desires and yours and how they align and if they do not." Until that moment, I had not considered that the mystics who believed they could be in unity with the Lord through

---

16 Philippians 2:13
17 Matthew 6:10

contemplation and self-surrender had a God that was fighting on their behalf, for them to embrace who he made them to be.

Let my testimony reassure you that he will pursue you when you get off track. He won't let you stay stuck for long. No one wants us to fulfill our destiny more than the Lord.

Around that time, I was reading the book of Acts. The Lord highlighted something to me. Paul was in Caesarea and a prophet came and told him his fate. When the people heard this and believed harm would come to him, they argued with him to stay where he would be safe. He was determined to go and would not change his mind, so they "gave up and said 'The Lord's will be done.'"[18] It was a prayer of concession. It was a prayer that meant they would stop arguing with the stubborn man and put it in the hands of the God they trusted.

They gave up.

God doesn't want prayers of concession. Sometimes, concession is necessary, but he gave us free will for a reason. He wants willing surrender, not for us to give up grudgingly. God wants us to choose.
He wants us to wrestle.

He wants us to reign[19] with Jesus, remember? You can't rule or reign without being a decision-maker. The testing we go through gives us wisdom and experience to make the right choices. It gives us the opportunity to be formed into the correct heart posture. God doesn't want us to try to return to him the free will that he gave us. He gave it to us for a reason. Forced love isn't true love.

God wants us to be ourselves. If he wanted obedient robots, he would have made robots. He made dynamic, creative, inventive humans in his image to create with him. He doesn't want slaves that do things for him.

---

18 Acts 21:14
19 Revelation 20:4; 2 Timothy 2:12

He wants friends who do things *with* him. Friends have opinions. They ask for favors. They help you when you move. They have feelings and make you go outside your comfort zone. They celebrate your kids. You like them because of their personalities. You like them for helping you grow and bringing new ideas to the table. You like spending time with them and creating memories. You enjoy shared experiences together, like watching new movies and chatting around bonfires. You argue with friends and challenge each other. You give and receive. You like who they are, and they like you. You like being imperfect, wonderful, funny, raw, and vulnerable together.

God *likes* you and *wants* to be your friend.
He wants friends who wrestle with him and ask for things and join him on his crazy adventures.
He wants friends to spend time with, who will bring a little more of him into the world.
He says, "Come with me," to us.
He wants friends who say, "Come with me," in return.

He wants to be invited.

Jesus, come be with me while I read.
Lord, come eat with us and bless our food.
Holy Spirit, come write this song, this book, this card with me.
Father, come tuck the kids you gave me into bed with me.
Holy Spirit, come speak to me while I watch this movie.
Lord, come to work with me.
Jesus, come back.

Love is active and passionate. Love reaches back and invites. Friend-ship is not one-sided. Friends must reach out to each other in order to keep the relationship alive. The Lord is constantly pursuing you, but in order for you to be in communion with him, you must reach back.

When you can't hear him, or he feels far away, you can always read about him. There is a whole book written about him and by him. Don't forget, the

Bible is one long love story. This collection of books tells the history of the underdog and how God plans to woo them after giving them free will. It's epic. Reading the Bible is like reading a personal love letter of all he's done to win our hearts even after humanity rejected him, rebelled against him, and killed his son.

The Bible is full of stories about lives consumed by big mistakes and how God loved, forgave, and redeemed those people. Over and over, it reflects how God pursued and wooed his people and didn't let them leave their walls up. He is kind. He is worthy. He is with us. He understands our frame[20] and knows we live in the tension of the present. He knows we can contend for a better future only so long before we burn out. He is way more aware of our needs than we ever will be. He always pursues and always forgives.

There was a man named Jonah who got a direct command from the Lord to go to a specific place, to a specific people, and tell them a message. Jonah refused. He tried to run from the Lord, from his presence, and he got on a boat to flee to another town. On the journey, the Lord sent an awful storm and the boat was about to be destroyed from the tempest. The men on the boat did all they could to stay alive, but after casting lots, they found the storm had risen against them because of this man Jonah. Jonah admitted he was running from the Lord, and he told them to throw him overboard. Jonah could have repented and agreed to go to Nineveh. The storm probably would have stopped. Instead, Jonah decided he would rather die.

The men throw him overboard, but God prevents him from drowning by having a great fish swallow him. Jonah is so stubborn, he spends three days and three nights in the belly of the fish before he even speaks to the Lord. As soon as he says he will fulfill his vow to the Lord and obey God, the fish spits him out on dry land.

Then, the Lord repeats himself. He commands Jonah, "Go to Nineveh, that evil city, and tell them to repent." This time, Jonah goes. He tells the people, "Repent or your city will be overthrown!" The people believe his message. They believe him to be speaking words from God. "They called for a fast

---

20 Psalm 103:14

and put on sackcloth, from the greatest of them to the least of them."[21] They fasted and mourned and asked God to relent from his judgement of their wicked deeds. The king even commanded that no person or animal should drink water, but that every living creature must fast all food and all drink. He commanded that they "call out mightily to God. Let everyone turn from his evil way and from the violence that is in his hands...When God saw what they did, how they had turned from their evil way, God relented of the disaster that he had said he would do them."[22]

This made Jonah furious. He says, "You are a gracious God and merciful, slow to anger and abounding in steadfast love, and relenting from disaster."[23] That may sound like a compliment, but Jonah was calling God a softy.

Jonah cried out to his friend, "I knew it! I know you! I knew you would back out of your threat and I would look dumb because I told them you would do something and you're not going to follow through! I look like a false prophet! I knew you'd do this to me! This is why I ran away and didn't want to go in the first place! They were so evil, and all they do is call a fast, and you're going to forgive them! They deserve your wrath, not your forgiveness! I would rather die than watch them live!"

God replies, "Does it benefit you to be angry?"

Angry Jonah goes and sits outside the city to see if he's right and if the Lord will relent and not harm it. While he sits to watch, a plant shades and comforts him, but the next day, it dies and he feels faint from the sun and wind beating down on him.

He cries out to the Lord in his misery, "Please let me die. It would be better for me to die than live."

But God replies again, "Does it benefit you to be this angry about a plant?"

---

[21] Jonah 3:5
[22] Jonah 3:8-10
[23] Jonah 4:2

He stubbornly says, "Yes, I do well to be angry, angry enough to die."[24]

Then God sets the record straight, "Let's be clear, Jonah. You want to die because you're angry about a plant. A plant which you did not cultivate, did not water, did not make grow. You care this much about a plant that only lived for a day. Should I not care even more for a great city for which I did labor, and did make grow, with many lives in it? They didn't know what they were doing and didn't know their sin, but now that you've told them, they do. They repented and fasted. They paused their lives to seek me. Should I not care even more for them?"

Checkmate.

That's how the story ends, with God's gentle rebuke.

In this story, God isn't just forgiving Nineveh. God forgives stubborn and angry Jonah, over and over. Even though Jonah does not fast or repent. God could have given up on Jonah. He could have told Jonah he was being stubborn or an immature child throwing a temper tantrum. He didn't have to explain himself to Jonah at the end. He could have let him die, or live in misery. But Jonah is God's friend and God doesn't give up on his friends. He's all in. He pursues Jonah, even when he's cranky. He saves Jonah from death. He saves him from misery. He prevents him from missing out on saving over 120,000 people. He demands Jonah live his best life, and he doesn't let him sit in his anger. He challenges him, and he knows exactly what Jonah needs to move in the right direction.

When we're friends with God, even when we rebel, try to throw our lives away, or ignore him, he pursues us. He does not give up on us. He is calling out for people to turn to him and run with him into the next epic adventure he has planned for their lives.

I wonder what Jonah and God did together next.

---

[24] Jonah 4:9

The Bible is also full of stories of people pouring out their lives and love and affection for the Lord. One particular story is repeated in all four gospels.[25] It says one night there was a dinner at Simon's house in Jesus' honor. Jesus was reclining at the table and a woman entered, looking for Jesus. Her name was Mary. Mary broke a bottle of the finest perfume, and poured out its entirety on Jesus. She anointed his head and feet with this jar of alabaster oil, while weeping and kissing his feet, washing them with her tears, and wiping them with her hair.

This is a scandalous scene. This public display of worship captures the attention of everyone in the building. It's a distracting, smelly scene. The room can't not notice a woman weeping, it's loud. They can't not notice the perfume being poured out; it's pungent. They can't not notice she poured out the whole bottle, it's extravagant. They can't not be appalled that this woman's behavior is publicly humiliating; it's offensive. She is kissing his feet, and she won't stop, and Jesus is letting her. Many in the room are indignant at the sight.

In their indignation, they rebuke and judge the woman and Jesus. First, they can't believe the waste of costly oil. "It could have been sold for more than a year's wages!"[26] The people harshly rebuke her and tell her there are so many other things a year's wages could have gone towards. She could have sold the pint of oil and given the money to the poor. That would have been better, they think. Second, this woman is a known prostitute. Simon, the Pharisee and host of the party, says to himself, "If this man were a prophet, he would have known who and what sort of woman this is who is touching him."[27] He's sure if Jesus knew, he wouldn't let her do such a thing. He deduces that since Jesus is letting her, he must not know, and since he doesn't know, he must not be a prophet or the Messiah.

To everyone's surprise, Jesus justifies her behavior. "'Leave her alone,' said Jesus. 'Why are you bothering her?'"[28] He explains that the poor will always be with them, but that his time is running out. In fact, his death is right

---

25 Matthew 26:6-13; Mark 14:3-9; John 12:1-8; Luke 7:36-50
26 Mark 14:5
27 Luke 7:39
28 Mark 14:6

around the corner and she is anointing him for burial. He declares it is a beautiful thing she's done for him. She was running out of time to love him in this way.

Then, knowing Simon's thoughts, Jesus directly challenges him with a parable:
> "'A certain moneylender had two debtors. One owed five hundred denarii, and the other fifty. When they could not pay, he cancelled the debt of both. Now which of them will love him more?' Simon answered, 'The one, I suppose, for whom he cancelled the larger debt.' And he said to him, 'You have judged rightly.' Then turning toward the woman he said to Simon, 'Do you see this woman? I entered your house; you gave me no water for my feet, but she has wet my feet with her tears and wiped them with her hair. You gave me no kiss, but from the time I came in she has not ceased to kiss my feet. You did not anoint my head with oil, but she has anointed my feet with ointment. Therefore I tell you, her sins, which are many, are forgiven—for she loved much. But he who is forgiven little, loves little.'"[29]

Mary of Bethany made a big mess of her life, but she also made a big mess in her love. Snot and tears and alabaster oil and hair enveloped the dirty feet that had walked all day in a first-century world. She went all-in with Jesus. She didn't hold back. She was honestly vulnerable, exposed not only to him, but shameless in her love. She displayed it publicly. She loved much because she knew her past and therefore, how much he had forgiven and redeemed her.

Mary didn't let the way the physical world saw her behavior stop her. She didn't cave to the expectations of her culture. She looked with spiritual eyes and acted in love. She knew living for Jesus' eyes alone was all that really mattered, and that everything else was meaningless.[30] Her act of extravagant love left an impression on the Lord, and on everyone else. Jesus honors Mary's memory and declares, "Wherever this gospel is preached

---
29 Luke 7:41-47
30 Ecclesiastes 2:15

throughout the world, what she has done will also be told, in memory of her."[31] I'm sure this event was unforgettable. It didn't matter that it was messy, that's what made it memorable. It was worth it. Her love left a legacy.

Will your messy love leave a legacy?

If that is your goal, the first step is to receive the greatest love of all. "Greater love has no one than this, that someone lay down his life for his friends."[32] Jesus is the greatest friend you'll ever have. He loved you first, and loves you most. Then, let's be like Mary, and be a friend of Jesus, who loves him in return, extravagantly.

Jesus made himself a fool, dying on a cross. Mary made herself a fool, in a public display of messy love. No one will be willing to love like Mary for a master or slave-driver. This kind of love is poured out on the lover of your soul, your dearest and most intimate friend. An extravagant act like this is reserved for Jesus, the one who came so you might have abundant life.[33]

A deep, intimate friendship with the Lord takes time. It takes vulnerability. It requires wrestling with how to live on the line between his reality and our reality. It takes commitment to see the world through his eyes. It takes communion.

Before Mary poured out her oil on his feet, she wrestled with his love for her. In the Gospel of John, he tells us how Mary's brother was sick and she and her sister called for Jesus to come heal him. Jesus didn't come. He let Lazarus die. When Jesus finally shows up, days later, Mary won't go to him. She's upset and offended. She's probably thinking, "Now?! How could you not come before? I thought we were your friends! I thought you loved us."

Her sister goes first and then tells Mary that Jesus is calling for her.[34] She goes quickly to meet him, but falls at his feet, literally falling apart. She

---
31 Matthew 26:13; Mark 14:9
32 John 15:13
33 John 10:10
34 Which might have been a good-natured lie from an older sister who wanted Mary to do the right thing. The Bible doesn't say Jesus asked for her. But, it doesn't say a lot of things Jesus did....

cries, "'Lord, if you had been here, my brother would not have died.' When Jesus saw her weeping, and the Jews who had come with her also weeping, he was deeply moved in his spirit and greatly troubled."[35]

Jesus weeps with Mary. Her tears and her love move him. Her faith and knowledge of what he could have done for her, and his not yet doing it, troubles him. Their friendship makes a difference in his connection to her.

Jesus planned all along to raise Lazarus from the dead. He intentionally delayed so that a miracle could be done. He tells his disciples this before he travels to the sisters. But he doesn't minimize her pain. He doesn't tell her to stop crying. He weeps with her. He is present with her in her pain before he asks to be taken to the tomb. Then, he resurrects her brother who's been dead for four days.

Jesus raises things from the dead for his friends.
He weeps with them and feels their pain.
He also defends their messy love.

May you be inspired by Mary to seek and know him, intimately. May you pour out your love at his feet. Love much, knowing you have been forgiven much. After all, "the greatest thing you'll ever learn is just to love and be loved in return."[36]

All you have to do is ask.

---

35 John 11:32-33
36 *Moulin Rouge!* Directed by Baz Luhrmann. Madrid, Spain: Twentieth Century Fox, 2001.

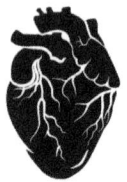

Invitation to Prayer

Jesus, I want to be your friend.
Please let me receive your love, and teach me how to love you in return.
I want my love for you, others, and myself, to leave a legacy. Help me to believe my messes and mistakes will bring me into a beautiful and passionate love for you and life.

I want to make a positive impact on the world around me.
I want to bring your love and your presence into the world.
I want to see this messy world with your eyes. Help me embrace the tension of living in both the spiritual and the physical.
I want to abide in you and still be present to the world around me. I don't want to escape or run away from pain, nor do I want to get sucked into it.
Give me hope in the midst of the storms of life.
Show me how you want me to engage both heaven and earth.

Lord, give me the desires of my heart.
In areas where I know what I want, open doors. In areas where you know what's best, and you know my desires are temporary and foolish, save me from myself. Show me what is best for me. Let me taste and see your goodness in answered and unanswered prayers.
Lead me into the highest and best path you have for my life.

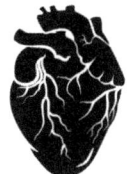

I have faith you want to be my closest friend.
Please, be my friend and let me be yours.
I want to be myself around you. I want you to speak and guide me like you are speaking to a friend. I don't want walls or pretense blocking honest vulnerability in our relationship.

Thank you for loving me where I am, and for your patience in all the areas I need to grow and become more like you.
Thank you for never giving up on me. Thank you for pursuing me like Jonah and weeping with me like Mary. Thank you for walking with me through all the ups and downs of life.
Increase my love for you.
Amen.

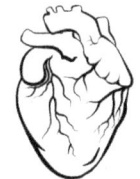

Step-by-Step

The Spring of 2018 marked my nine-year anniversary of being an entrepreneur and wedding planner. I had grown a successful business, working with elite and destination couples planning their memorable events in New Mexico. I was starting to build a reputation throughout the Rocky Mountain region and develop business in nearby states. I was ready to grow from "Best in New Mexico" to "Best in the Southwest."

There was only one problem. I was hearing God say he wanted me to take a very different next step. I was hearing that he wanted me to shut it down. I felt like God was saying I wouldn't be around, maybe that I would be elsewhere, or wouldn't be available to plan weddings. That didn't make sense. Both my husband and my business were location-based. Our families were there. We had just bought a home. We were established and rooted in Albuquerque. There was no reason to move and no logical reason to quit what I was doing.

While God was making this "first step" to follow him clear, anything following felt vague. Every time a new couple inquired, this feeling would nudge me again, and I'd decline the event. It haunted me until I fully obeyed. I was feeling this consistent nudge from the Lord and I couldn't ignore him. I was fully booked throughout 2018, but I started declining all business for 2019 and beyond.

At the same time, my husband and I were meeting with marriage counselors. Things were going downhill fast, and my counselor pulled me aside to recommend we separate. That's when the very controversial next step arrived. God agreed with her. I heard him say, "I want you to leave."

I only pushed back a little about closing my business. I was resistant, but not argumentative. I trusted there were other ways to make money. But when God is encouraging divorce, you question if you're actually hearing him. I fought a lot. I argued. I prayed. I sought counsel. I told him I couldn't be hearing him right. I told him Bible verses he should know. I did everything in my power to convince him his directions were wrong. I wanted him to fix things. I reminded him that I made a vow, to him! He should know that. After lots of wrestling, I finally consented, "Lord if you want this, you have to make him ask me to move out. He has to initiate it, so I know it's you."

My husband asked me to move out. Within a month, I was living with my Mom and I had no more weddings on my calendar. I was jobless and getting a divorce. My calendar hadn't been that empty, ever.

Thank God it was empty though, because I couldn't do much. When I thought he might be cheating, I went to the doctor to get tested and received the HPV vaccine. To my unexpected dismay, I had an allergic reaction that sent my body into a full-blown rash for years. When you eat something or take a pill that leaves your system in a matter of hours, that reaction clears up quickly. But when you inject something into your body, there is no way to remove it. I was covered in hives from my cheeks to ankle. Doctors gave me steroid cream and told me to take allergy meds, but there was nothing they could do. My body wanted whatever had been put inside of it, out, and the fastest way to expel it was through my skin. I had to let it run its course.

The injection combined with the emotional stress of my business closing and marriage ending made it even worse. My physical body was overwhelmed. Any little thing, soaps, lotions, candles, anything with perfume, any self-care items, made the hives spread. Even standing in the heat of the sun would make it worse, like a blistering sunburn. My body was totally rejecting anything that made me feel loved or special. I was miserable emotionally and physically.

This is why I call 2018 my "Job season."

In the story of Job, Satan is prowling around the earth looking for someone to ruin. God brags to Satan about Job's integrity and Satan incites the Lord. Satan says Job is only friends with and worships God because he's blessed him. He tells God, "If you take away his blessings and his health, he'll curse you." God gives Satan permission to test Job, knowing that Job will hold to his integrity and that their relationship is real. Satan takes Job's property and income and kills his 10 children and strikes him with painful sores from head to toe.[1]

My life mirrored the story of Job. It felt like God allowed the enemy to come take away my career and provision and all the things that brought me joy, including the people I loved and my health. I literally had painful oozing hives from head to toe. Satan has no new tricks. Many would have cursed God for their misfortune, but like Job, I turned to him for help. I cried out. After all, in my opinion, God was kinder to me than he was to Job. He had warned me early on that change was coming, months ahead of time. I suspected something bigger was going on. I knew he had a plan and I actually wondered what he was protecting me from. I wondered how much harder life would have been, had I not obeyed his direction.

I wanted to fill my empty schedule with quality time with Jesus. I reflected on the story of Abraham, and how he traveled to God only knows where, and returned to the place where he had last heard God's voice when he didn't know what to do. I thought to myself, "The last time I knew I was in the right place was in seminary." So I traveled to Oregon to retreat with the Lord and seek his direction.

---

[1] Job 1-2

I wrote a rough draft of this book and found peace in the midst of the mess. I prayed, journaled, self-reflected and repented, released things, laughed with the locals, and considered moving to live a simple life near the beach. That is, until I got a call from a potential wedding planning client. I felt that familiar nudge and knew another next step had appeared. I scheduled an interview and afterward, I heard, "Take the job."

"What?! I thought you wanted me to close the business! You said no when I got inquiries for August and October. Why for this random September wedding, do you say yes? You make no sense."

I was confused, but I strongly felt I was supposed to book the wedding. I genuinely enjoyed them and thought I would love working with them, so I was thrilled to get a divine green light. I emotionally and mentally shrugged, and I wondered if God was going to lead me back to wedding planning.

Two months later, I was still waiting for the next step. I went to church and a prophetic woman called me out of the crowd. I mentioned this moment to you in the first chapter. This woman was a stranger and knew nothing about my life. First, she told me she saw the Lord giving me a pearl necklace for all the hardship I'd been through over the last few difficult years. She was reminded of the verse, "Do not throw your pearls before pigs, lest they trample them underfoot and turn to attack you."[2] It seemed to communicate that I had been offering my pearls, the treasures nearest and dearest to my heart, to those who didn't appreciate them. They had been trampled on and destroyed, and God was redeeming me. He was handing me a new set of pearls to replace what had been destroyed. God also showed her a picture of a paintbrush in my hand, and a can of paint in the other labeled the color of "change." She felt like God was saying, it is time to paint a new life. When I sat down, the next step arrived. I heard, "Go to the prayer room."

This step was completely unexpected. I had heard of the prayer room in Kansas City, but I didn't really know anything about it. I found out the ministry was offering a scholarship for interns. Moving across the country

---

2 Matthew 7:6

is a big step, so I wasn't going to assume the scholarship was what God meant when he said, "Go to the prayer room." Instead, I saw they had a week-long event, similar to a retreat. I felt the familiar nudge again, "Go."

The benefit of having a clear calendar is that I could obey.
I had no obligations.
So, I bought a ticket, hopped in the car, and drove to Kansas City.

You would think God would've talked to me about my divorce while I was there. Surely, I needed some crisis intervention, right? Apparently not. The most monumental thing that week was an unexpected curve ball from years before. God showed me that I hadn't dealt internally with my belief that my Dad derailed my life path when he prevented me from going into ministry when I was eighteen. That issue had caused deeply rooted pain and fear and unforgiveness. That gunk had been poisoning my purpose. It had caused me to bury and try to forget about what Jesus had asked me to do: "Tell the world I love them."

When I realized all this, I wept at the state of my heart. I mourned my lost years, forgave my Dad, and committed myself to seeking a better way. This is what we call Godly sorrow[3] and repentance in Christianity. The sin itself had caused enough harm in my own life. I had already learned my lesson. I didn't need any chastisement. When I released this spiritual gunk to the Lord, I felt like a tree had been uprooted from my soul. I'd never felt so empty and so hungry for the truth.

After a week of Holy Spirit encounters, revelations like that one, teachings about finding our identity in Christ, and hours in the prayer room, I was feeling refreshed. However, all week long, I had been asking about that scholarship. No one knew the answers to my questions.

On the very last day, someone came to speak to our class about the scholarship and explained how it was an internship and ministry training program scheduled at night. It required living a simple life for a season, focusing on prayer and detaching yourself from the common concerns of

---
3   2 Corinthians 7:10–11

daily life. I didn't feel the familiar nudge. Unlike all the other steps leading up to this step, I didn't need a nudge. I had wanted this since I was eighteen.

At every other step along the way, it was as if I had walked up to a door, and God said open it. This time, it seemed like I was standing at a door, and there was no other door in sight, so I knocked. I figured if I was meant to go through it, God would open the door. With my divorce looming in the background, I was certain they wouldn't accept me and my mess. I was certain if this was what the Lord wanted, he would have to get involved. I applied and assumed the door would not open. It was past the deadline and they said thousands of people had applied for only one hundred openings. I had a long list of physical reasons to believe this door would not open.

As you already know, I was wrong. God opened the door. I was packing up my belongings and moving across the country only two months later. God was picking me up out of my old life and placing me in a new one. I had nothing left to lose. I might as well start over somewhere new.

Only then, once time had passed and things began to unfold, did God's instructions from a year prior make complete sense. "You won't be here" and "you won't be able to plan weddings" were previously inconceivable. He had hinted at and prepared me for all the things I couldn't foresee with his perfect leadership. If I had fought him and resisted, or demanded to see why before I acted, I would have been off schedule with his plan.
Even the one wedding that God told me to book was perfectly timed. That very weekend in September was the one and only week-long break during the internship. And, that one and only wedding would be just enough income to support my whole adventure. Because I listened and obeyed, everything worked out seamlessly.

Now, here's the ironic part.

Do you remember what I told you I wanted before moving?

I was asking myself, "I focused solely on God, would he really, actually, take care of everything else?"

Is it clear to anyone else that he sure seemed to be taking care of everything *before* I moved to Kansas City?

I didn't need to lavish my undivided attention on him in a prayer room for eight hundred hours to get him to love or like me. He already liked and loved me. I didn't need to move across the country to be told the next step. He guided my every step along the way.

I was seeking what I already had.

Honestly, I didn't appreciate God nearly as much as I should have. I wasn't very thankful for his help during my mess. I felt like my life had crumbled and been burned to the ground that year. I was confused and tired and angry and grieving. I was like a wild animal trying to bite and scratch its rescuer. But the truth is, while my life circumstances were imperfect, God was good and led me step-by-step to exactly where I needed to be.

He led me out of my financial dependence on the wedding industry just in time, right before the COVID pandemic stole it from all my friends and previous coworkers.

He led me away from a man who defined love differently than I do.
He gave me enough money to live on during my Nightwatch adventure, and then beyond, through COVID.
He took care of *everything*: past, present, and future.

God always had taken care of everything, and he always will. He doesn't change.[4] His timing is and always was perfect. My focus on him didn't increase his favor in my life. I already had his unwavering favor.

There's a wonderful and funny clip of Heidi Baker telling a story about when she first met the prophet Bob Jones.[5] She talks about how she had fasted one-third of her life without understanding the heart of the Lord.

---
4 Psalm 33:11
5 I suggest you pause reading and go listen to it for 10 minutes, seriously! MorningStar Ministries, "Have a Cookie – Heidi Baker," YouTube video, posted November 24, 2017, https://youtu.be/RVfg7ZnCQQw

When she met the prophet, he said the word of the Lord to her was, "Eat a cookie." Through her funny and moving antics, she shares how the Lord crashed in on her while she ate a freshly baked, chocolate chip cookie. She heard God say, "You're not an orphan. You don't have to starve to get my favor. You have my favor."[6] When she finishes eating the cookie, still in tears, Bob gleefully tells her, "Eat another one."[7] Through two extravagant, sweet treats, Heidi touched the heart of the Father. She experienced his goodness and kindness and love. She says it changed her life.

Aside from Heidi's testimony, one of the many stories in the Bible that proves we have unwavering favor is the parable of the prodigal son.[8] In the story, a wealthy man's son asks for his inheritance early and goes to squander his wealth in reckless living. He lives it up for a while, enjoying great food and beautiful women. Then things take an unexpected turn for the worst. Famine hits the land and he's forced into work feeding pigs. He's so hungry in the famine, he wishes he could eat the pig slop. He has officially hit rock bottom.

From rock bottom, he can see how amazing life was with his family. He remembers and appreciates what he had before, and how even the hired help was fed well and treated with dignity. He decides to return home and ask his father to be a hired hand. He believes he doesn't deserve to be a son anymore because of what he's done, but even as a slave, he knows would be treated better in his father's house than out in the world.

When he returns home, his father is watching for him. When he is still far off, the father recognizes him, has compassion on him, and runs to him. When they meet, the son starts repenting and confessing he's no longer worthy, but the father cuts him off. He doesn't even let him finish. The father calls to his other servants and says, "Bring him the family credit card, and new clothes, and new shoes. We're going to throw a party and celebrate that my son has returned!"

---

6 Ibid. 7:36
7 Ibid. 8:19
8 Luke 15:11-32

When the Father gives him a robe and a ring and puts new shoes on his feet, he's restoring his son's dignity. He turns him away from rebellion and slavery and restores him to sonship. He re-establishes him to his rightful place. He restores his birthright. The Father does not let a season of rebellion ruin their relationship.

Jesus tells this story to show us the heart of the Father, God. We don't acquire God's love through works. We don't need to be perfect or strive. This parable shows how God will respond to our weak efforts to come near to him, or do the right thing. While we are still far away, he runs to our aid. The father doesn't hesitate to lavish love on the prodigal son.

When we believe God is good and safe, just like this father, we know we can return home to him and he will embrace us with open arms. God's love and kindness is meant to draw us into repentance.[9] He doesn't hold our past, our weakness, or our failures against us. He doesn't withhold himself from us. God loves to bring dignity to our identity and guide us back on a path that leads to living life abundantly.

God was not waiting for my life to be perfect to intervene. He was not holding my sin over my head. He had led me for years, meeting me right where I was, in my mess. His heart was to do life with me, step-by-step.

That is God's heart for you too.

In another example of the heart of God, John tells a story about a woman who was caught in adultery.[10] The teachers of religious law and the Pharisees bring her to Jesus and say, "Now in the Law, Moses commanded us to stone such women. So what do you say?"[11] Jesus responds by stooping down and writing in the dust with his finger. He doesn't say a word. They keep pressing him, so he rises to say, "Let him who is without sin among you be the first to throw a stone."[12] He bends down again to write. They "went away one by one, beginning with the older ones."[13] When they were

9 Romans 2:4
10 John 8:1-11
11 John 8:5
12 John 8:7
13 John 8:9

all gone, it was just her and Jesus. Jesus says to her, "'Woman, where are they? Has no one condemned you?' She said, 'No one, Lord.' And Jesus said, 'Neither do I condemn you; go, and from now on sin no more.'"[14]

The religious leaders tested God to see if he would follow through with the law as they understood it. Jesus chose love over religion and convicted every one of their own sin. He proved to them that they were no more righteous than she, and declared forgiveness and freedom over her. He didn't need to chastise or convict her of her sin. She was thoroughly convinced what she did was wrong. The sin itself had caused enough harm and public humiliation. She had already learned her lesson. God didn't punish her. The effect of the sin was penalty enough.

In the beginning, there was only one rule, one law on the Earth. The law was, "You may surely eat of every tree of the garden, but of the tree of the knowledge of good and evil you shall not eat, for in the day that you eat of it you shall surely die."[15] God gave clear and easy instructions. "You have freedom to eat from any tree, except this one, because it will kill you." Just like a good parent, out of his love for them and desire to protect them, he gave instructions to avoid doing the one thing that would cause them harm.

Even in the beginning, there was one determined to challenge the goodness of God and the good intentions of his rules. In the garden, the serpent came to Eve to debate what God really meant when he gave his instruction. He debated how that one law should be followed, or if it was really to their benefit to obey God.

"He said to the woman, 'Did God actually say, "You shall not eat of any tree in the garden?"' And the woman said to the serpent, 'We may eat of the fruit of the trees in the garden, but God said, "You shall not eat of the fruit of the tree that is in the midst of the garden, neither shall you touch it, lest you die."'"[16]

---

14 John 8:9-11
15 Genesis 2:16
16 Genesis 3:1-3

In this first part, the serpent exaggerates the law and asks Eve if God is not allowing her to eat any of the fruit in the garden. It's a typical exaggeration, "If you can't have one, you can't have any." His question implies God is harsh and stingy. In her reply, Eve could have repeated God's law word for word, but she does not. She does the same thing the serpent did, just a little differently. She has her own exaggeration, "If I can't have it, I can't even touch it."

But that's not true. God didn't say don't touch it. He said don't eat it.

If she touches it, she won't die. Only if she eats it, will she die. Eve added her personal guidelines to the guidelines of the Lord, and made that her law. It seems her rule of thought was, "To avoid eating it, I better not touch it." That might be convincing at first, but when she touches it and doesn't die, she'll question the whole law, not just the secret sauce she added.

When Eve misquotes the Lord in this way, the serpent is able to turn it on her. Her enemy is crafty and he knows that eating the fruit won't cause instantaneous death. "You will not surely die. God knows that when you eat of it your eyes will be opened, and you will be like God, knowing good and evil."[17] The serpent is accusing God of keeping something from her. He continues to challenge God's goodness and is apparently able to convince her that being like God and knowing both good and evil is better. He convinces Eve that God is against her. The truth is, God is for her, and his rules are for her benefit. If she trusted God was good, she would have believed there was a good reason to obey him. If she believed there was a good reason, she would not need to fully understand God's way to obey.

The serpent twists the truth. He entices her with a lie she doesn't fully understand. It's true she won't die instantaneously, physically. Not if she touches it; not if she eats it. If she never eats it, she will never know death. If she eats it, she will die. Instantly, the act of sin will separate her from God, and that disconnection will be spiritual death to her heart and soul. Eventually, her physical mind and body will give out as well. If she eats it, her eyes will be opened, but not in the way she thinks. No, she will lose her

---

17 Genesis 3:4-5

childlike innocence. She doesn't know it is this childlike innocence that connects her to the heart of the Lord and brings her abundant life.

Eve goes and picks the fruit. She touches it and doesn't die. She eats it and doesn't breathe her last. She hands it to her husband, and he eats it and doesn't collapse. If the serpent was right, they would have gone and found God and told him he was wrong. "We ate it and didn't die, God. Why did you lie to us?"

No, something worse happens. The moment Adam and Eve ate the fruit of the tree of the knowledge of good and evil, their eyes were opened to see evil. They saw their sin. They saw their lack of goodness, compared to the holy God. They recognized in their disobedience that they were prideful and doubted God's goodness. They felt shame for the first time. They hid from the Lord. Previously, in their childlike innocence, they drew near to him.[18] They were not aware of their shame or nakedness or vulnerability. They did not know evil. But once they were aware of the evil within and could compare themselves to God and others, as being more or less good or more or less evil, this knowledge disconnected them from God.[19]

It is a really sad story. It's a story of a father who loves his children so much that he gives them the freedom to stay near him or run away from him. They are tricked into doubting his love for them and it leads to them running away. Their connection to the source and Creator of all life was to live, but eating the fruit of the tree disconnects them from the source of their breath and life. It brings death.

The enemy uses this same old trick today. He wants people to believe that God is against them, that he's not good, that he's only trying to prevent people from experiencing enlightenment that comes from uninhibited freedom to do and say and be whatever they want. He loves to lie and accuse God of being a killjoy. He whispers lies to convince people that the thing they desire, the thing that God said would cause harm, will bring them life;

---

18 I wonder if Jesus had this in mind when he said we needed to be like children. "Truly, I say to you, unless you turn and become like children, you will never enter the kingdom of heaven." Matthew 18:3
19 Genesis 3:8

when the truth is, it only brings death. Death is rarely instantaneous; sin is most often a slow death.

When someone considers adultery, it might not instantaneously kill their marriage, but it will slowly fade into suffocating their marriage with the fantasy of an affair, long before the affair may actually occur. The sin happens in the heart, way before it is acted out in the body. The lie the enemy whispers is that the grass is greener outside the boundary of marriage.

When someone is disrespectful to and ungrateful for their parents, it might not instantaneously kill their relationship, but repeated behavior will be a slow fade into disowning each other. Dishonoring them will only cause division and destroy the family. The lie the enemy whispers is that we are wiser and better than our parents, that their imperfection makes them unworthy of our love or kindness.

When someone is afraid of lack or compares themselves with others based on materialism, and begins to give up their sabbath, their rest, to acquire more and more things, their worship of money and things will become more important than investing in their family. Years later, they will find themselves alone and abounding in things that do not satisfy them. If they are finally willing to trade all those things for the love they actually want, it may be too late to rebuild those relationships.

When someone longs for intimacy and love, but instead of seeking a mate for life, they settle for the instant gratification of porn, they train their bodies to respond to and desire this imitation. But since the human heart was meant for a creative, dynamic, ever-changing relationship with a sexual partner, their body will get bored of videos. They will try new videos and more videos to fulfill the part that's missing. This cheap imitation of intimacy can become so deeply ingrained into the body, that over time the body will no longer respond to sexual intimacy with a partner. The body will be trained out of the natural desire to receive love and experience sexual connection. This too, is a slow fade, and it may be the scariest of all.

What does God say about all these things?

"I say to you that everyone who looks at a woman with lustful intent has already committed adultery with her in his heart."[20]

"Pride goes before destruction, and a haughty spirit before a fall."[21]

"If a man offered for love all the wealth of his house, he would be utterly despised."[22]

"Flee from sexual immorality. Every other sin a person commits is outside the body, but the sexually immoral person sins against his own body."[23]

In all of these examples, what is initially perceived as freedom, ends in death and loss. God warns us, directly, to avoid all of these situations (and many others) in the Bible. He wants us to enjoy an abundant life, and warns us that our choices are the hinge between life and death.

Do you heed his warning? Will you listen? Will you obey? Or do you rage against God, believing the instant gratification you want now, your way, is worth slowly suffocating something to death?

Psalm 2 speaks about how the nations, all people, rage against the Lord and his son's leadership, and will until Jesus returns. It speaks of how people look at the instruction of the Lord as limiting and bondage, and wish to break away from his way to have what they think is freedom.[24] The Psalm ends with a warning to obey and submit to God's way. "Be wise...serve the Lord with fear...blessed are those who take refuge in him."[25] Psalm 2 says it is wise to follow and trust the Lord so you do not perish, and instead, live a blessed life.

It's really amazing how much the Lord warns us, in his Word, to prevent us from ruining our lives with choices that kill, steal, or destroy. God gives us simple wisdom to live an abundant life. Even more amazing, when we don't heed him and instead, we choose to make a decision that destroys a part of our life, God receives us back with open arms. God truly is like the father in

---

20 Matthew 5:28
21 Proverbs 16:18
22 Song of Solomon 8:7
23 1 Corinthians 6:18
24 Psalm 2:1-3
25 Psalm 2:10-12

the story, who runs to his son and restores his dignity when the son returns home. Like Jesus did with the woman who committed adultery, he will comfort us and say, "Wasn't that awful? Go live your life and don't do this again."

God was for us and gave us everything we needed to know to make good choices before we got here. Then, Jesus died to pay for all the bad ones we make. So, if we do make a bad choice, one that leads to death, we can call upon him and ask for his help, and he will exchange that death for a new life.

Sometimes, it's not our choice that leads to death, but the choices of the people around us. In the examples above, the family is affected by the person who chooses lust, materialism, or pride. In these situations, it's not just the individual who needs to exchange death for life, it's the family who was affected.

We all need Jesus. We all need to exchange death for life. Jesus wants to walk through life with us, step-by-step, and breathe life into every choice, every day.

When I think back on all the death that consumed my life in 2018, and how God led me step-by-step away from the destruction, I'm so grateful for his good leadership. I didn't know my little world was burning down around me. I didn't know how my choices, the choices of those around me, and the circumstances on the planet would lead to so much death and destruction in all our lives. Only God had the bird's-eye view and knew how to guide me step-by-step through the fires and away from them to safety.

Everyone seems to have their own unique way of hearing or feeling the Lord's direction. However you've learned to recognize his guidance, lean in. The Bible says those who belong to Jesus listen to him and follow him.[26] Often he only tells us what we need to know, today. We have to trust that in time, all things will be revealed.

---

26 John 10:27

If at the beginning of 2018, God dumped all the bad news on me at once, it would have crushed me. Can you imagine?

"You're going to be divorced in a few months, so I'm going to move you across the country. Then a worldwide pandemic is coming, and it's going to shut down the wedding industry, so start closing now, or you will lose everything."

That foresight would have crushed me! The small step-by-step instructions were best. Saying "Decline business, you're going to be busy doing something else," was all I needed to know to head in the right direction, and it didn't overwhelm me. I didn't fully understand what it meant, but it was enough.

If he told me I was standing in the midst of all those fires, I would have focused on the fire. Instead, God wants us to keep our eyes on him.[27] Clearly, God leading us step-by-step is his loving-kindness towards us. We think we want to know everything, but I'm sure it would break us. We have to trust that if it is good for us to know something, he will tell us at the perfect time.

Walking one step at a time with him for many years has led me to believe the step-by-step guidance is also one of the ways he exercises our trust in him. Jesus said that those who steward what they are given well, will be given abundantly more.[28]

If God tells you to do something, or not do something, it's because he wants to lead you to what is highest and best for you in life. He desires to give good gifts, and he desires to shield you from harm. He is good and wise and knows how to perfectly lead us through and away from the fires in our lives.

Whether he speaks to you directly, or it's straight from the Bible, there is a benefit to your obedience. You have his favor. His guidance is never to punish you. He is rooting for you and cheering you on, wanting you to live

---

27 Hebrews 12:1-2
28 Matthew 25:29

an abundant life of all the good things he has to offer. All good things come from him.[29]

Invite him to speak more, do more, and lead more.
Then, commit to listen more, respond more, and follow more.
He wants to be part of every step.
Plus, he just might surprise you as he infuses goodness into everything....

All you have to do is ask.

---

29 James 1:17

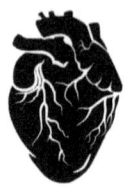

Invitation to Prayer

Lord, lead me. This world is messy. My life is messy. I've been more focused on the fires around me than you. Help me to see you in the midst of this mess. Open my eyes to see the ways I've settled for instant gratification and lies that are truly stealing from me, killing me, or destroying my life. Lead me step-by-step away from these traps, lead me into your loving arms.

Show me the heart of the Father; let me experience your love.

I'm asking you to redeem me. Bring me into a relationship with you where I feel and know what it means to be a son or daughter instead of a slave.

I don't want to be held captive by anything. I want to know deep in my bones that you are for me and I have your favor.

I want to know you forgive me and make me clean.

I want to experience running into your arms and feeling loved and accepted, more than I ever have by the things in this world.

I am asking for your freedom and your peace. I know I can't walk in these truths without your help.

Jesus, come help me. Clean out all the things that make big promises but don't satisfy. I want to live an abundant, joyful, wholehearted, fulfilling life with you. Live inside of me, through me. Show me how you are infusing goodness into my mess. Speak more, show me more, lead me more.

I commit to listen more, respond more, follow more.

I say yes to you, but you have to help me with all the rest, Jesus.

I can't do it without you.

Amen.

Spiritual Family

The religious leaders of Jesus' day were not very fond of him. They had rules about who was in and who was out of God's favor. They believed those who were paralyzed or blind or diseased had done something to deserve those punishments.[1] They had built a specific structure to assess who was righteous and who was a sinner.

When Jesus came, he flipped things upside down.

He spent time with the tax collectors and sinners and prostitutes instead of those who the temple deemed righteous. Instead of becoming what people wanted him to be, the next religious or military leader, Jesus rebelled against the system. He went his own way: God's way. Over time, the religious leaders became angrier and angrier at Jesus' way of doing things.

In Matthew's gospel, he gives us a picture of how things escalated.[2] Jesus goes from healing on the Sabbath to casting out demons and the crowds are amazed and starting to ask if he's the Messiah. To diminish his reputation, the religious leaders accuse Jesus of partnering with the prince of demons. Previously, Jesus didn't defend himself when they said things like this,[3] but

---

[1] One example is the disciples asking about this in John 9:1-3.
[2] Matthew 12:22-50
[3] Matthew 9:34

this time, he confronts them. He defends himself with common sense. He says that driving out demons by the power of demons would mean demons were divided against themselves, and that doesn't make any sense. He said any kingdom divided against itself will fall.

Jesus confronts their evil accusations. He says evil people produce bad fruit and good people produce good fruit, and that you can tell what a person is like on the inside by the fruit they produce. While he's still explaining how evil really works, how it moves in and takes over a person, someone approaches him to say, "Hey, your mother and brothers are standing outside, wanting to speak to you."

This person is really saying, "Hint, hint, you're embarrassing your family with your controversial teachings and how you're calling out the religious leaders. You can't say, 'I'm not partnering with Satan, you are the ones speaking evil, you brood of vipers!' to these people in power. It's dangerous, Jesus! Your family wants you to stop."

Jesus is not in the mood to placate. He knows he's risking his life with his words. He's aware of what he's doing. He's intentional. He motions to his disciples and replies to this messenger, "Here are my mother and my brothers! For whoever does the will of my Father in heaven is my brother and sister and mother."[4]

He's saying, these people:
who are pursuing the kingdom,
who desire to bring heaven on earth,
who open their hearts to love the Lord more and more,
who want to seek him and learn all they can,
who don't care about the rumors or the authorities disagreeing,
who stand by me when I speak truth and rebuke false teachers,
who left their old ways and old life to follow me,
this is my *family*.

---

[4] Matthew 12:49-50

These *same* people:
lacked faith and felt fear,[5]
needed to be taught just like everyone else,[6]
didn't know what Jesus was talking about half the time,[7]
struggled with comparison,[8]
caused trouble for him with the authorities,[9]
were super annoyed by people and complained,[10]
were so offended by others' lack of hospitality, they wanted to call down fire from heaven to destroy whole villages,[11]
and even tried to rebuke him or influence his behavior sometimes.[12]

Does this sound like anyone you know?
Just about everyone, right!?

Jesus' disciples weren't perfect; they were human! But their desire was to do the will of God, and Jesus proclaimed they did. They were sincere in their pursuit to love the Lord with all their heart, mind, and strength. Faith in Jesus enters you into his spiritual family.

Basic Christian teachings will tell you that the will of God is that you would believe in Jesus. The Bible actually says it is not only his will that you would be saved, but also, that you would be sanctified,[13] i.e. be made holy. While becoming holy is only possible through Jesus,[14] it will also take everything you have. It takes all of you, to empty yourself out and be refilled with his Spirit. To be filled with the Spirit is to embrace his will to bring the kingdom of heaven to earth.

This is a great mystery and paradox in Christianity. In one sense, we can do nothing. We cannot remove our pride in our own power. We cannot

---

5 Matthew 8:26; Matthew 14:46
6 Matthew 10
7 Matthew 13:36; Matthew 16:8-9
8 John 21:21
9 Matthew 12:2; Matthew 15:2
10 Matthew 15:23
11 Luke 9:54
12 Matthew 15:12; Matthew 16:22
13 1 Thessalonians 4:3-8
14 Hebrews 10:10

remove our own sins. We cannot even make ourselves love God more. Yet, in another sense, our free will means *active partnership with God is required for transformation.* We must render our desires and plans secondary to his. We must ask him to empty us of our selfish, earthly desires and refill them with heavenly desires. We must choose him and believe with faith that he will transform us. We must be willing to get close to the light that exposes all our darkness. We must be willing to be humbled and purified.

The Bible says we should offer our lives as a living sacrifice to the Lord[15] and obey him out of love.
It says what we do with our bodies (how we act) is considered worship, and we must worship him in spirit and in truth.[16]
In other words, our worship or lack thereof is infused into all we do.
The Bible says our offerings and sacrifices are a "pleasing aroma" to the Lord.

Humor me for a moment. Imagine that every action and every thought released a fragrance from your body...

What if every time you were thankful, you smelled jasmine or frankincense?
What if every time you were generous, you smelled olives and every time you laughed with joy, you smelled peaches?
What if every time you chose to be selfless, and acted loving or kind, you smelled flowers?
What if every time you chose to purify your thoughts, or asked for God to cleanse you, you smelled a mix of fresh rain and clean laundry?

Then, when you met someone new, you could say they smelled like flowers and fresh fruit instead of saying they were genuine and joyful and intentional.

Then, what if when you acted selfishly you smelled cat pee, and when you did something wrong even though you knew better, you smelled rotten eggs?

---
15 Romans 12:1
16 Romans 12:1; John 4:23-24

What if every time you had a lustful thought you smelled a wet dog? What if every time you got around someone who was in bondage to their addiction, you felt nauseous from their pungent aroma of alcohol or sweat or fried food?

The Lord sees and smells it all.
Sometimes we smell like roses,
and sometimes we smell like rotten eggs.

To those of you who are empathic or sense things in the spirit, you already pick up on this. You can feel or sense when a person is a creepy predator and can't be trusted. You can also sense when a person has a "sweet spirit" or an "old soul." It's as though you can pick up on the aroma they give off in the spiritual realm.

If this book has yet to convince you to prioritize spirituality over religion, now is the time.

To be spiritual means, "To be joined in spirit." It's a connection that is "affecting the spirit" or "related to sacred matters."[17] To be spiritually Christian then, is to be joined in spirit with Jesus.[18] It is to be in relationship and communion with him through listening, following, speaking, and obeying in a way that affects you emotionally, physically, mentally, and spiritually. It is to let Jesus and his way affect your spirit and to consider your relating to him to be a sacred matter.

If we are joined with Jesus, then his pleasing aroma, the aroma of Christ, permeates through us. In other words, "Our lives are a Christ-like fragrance rising up to God." (NLT)[19]

He smells like perfection, sacrificial love, kingship, sonship, joy, peace…and when we ask Jesus to come live inside us, he infuses us with himself. The most amazing part is that the aroma of Jesus highlights the best and unique

---

17 *Merriam-Webster.com Dictionary*, s.v. "spiritual," accessed May 26, 2021, https://www.merriam-webster.com/dictionary/spiritual.
18 John 17:21; 1 Corinthians 6:17
19 2 Corinthians 2:15; NLT.

parts of you. His aroma doesn't erase yours. It accentuates all the best smells and purifies all the bad ones.

Imagine your favorite smell.
It's better than that.

It's better than
    campfire and ocean
        or desert rain
            or pumpkin spice lattes in the fall.[20]

Christian culture encourages all the people who smell alike, i.e. think alike, to stay together. We've separated under many different teachers. You might align yourself with Calvin, Luther, conservatives, or liberals, but Jesus said he was the *only* one we should call teacher.[21]

It's like the tower of Babel[22] is still affecting us. Whoever speaks the same language still hangs out together. But the Lord said when the good news was preached to all people, all nations, all languages, then he would come back.[23] He wants us to spread his good aroma all over the earth. He doesn't want us to stay segregated from the world, or avoid different denominations that think differently than we do. He hates division. He desires a different kind of unity.

God sees the whole church, every denomination around the world, worshiping under the same blue sky. God loves our diversity. He created us to be different. The church is all who believe in Jesus, not just those who meet in a building, take part in a specific denomination, or express their worship in a specific way.

As someone who always felt set-apart and different, I'm personally acquainted with the feeling of not belonging. I sought to find where I might fit. My diverse Christian background taught me to color outside the lines.

---

20 Don't hate me, I couldn't help myself.
21 Matthew 23:8
22 Genesis 11
23 Matthew 24:14

Spiritual Family | 147

I don't quite fit in the lines of the conservative church, or the lines of the liberal church. I don't really fit in the lines of any denomination. I believe Jesus' way is somewhere in-between, and he's looking for those who will seek the narrow path and aim to walk in it.
I want to follow Jesus, not the church.

This is one of the reasons I claim to be a Christian Mystic. People who practice different kinds of mysticism might have hijacked this word, but I want to redeem it. The word mystic means, "A person who seeks by contemplation and self-surrender to obtain unity" with God and/or someone "who believes in the spiritual understanding of truths that are beyond the intellect."[24]

I like the word mystic because it hints at my belief that everything is spiritual, at a level humans can't intellectually comprehend. When I say everything is spiritual, I mean that the Bible doesn't separate the spiritual from the physical. Everything is connected. Your Spirit effects your body, effects your emotions, effects your thoughts, and those effect your spirit and so on, in a never ending cycle. You are completely interconnected. Nothing you do is only physical. Your actions are worship, they have an aroma, remember? As a mystic, I live and act with this in mind.

To say I'm Christian will invoke all kinds of definitions the listener has known about Christians, but when I add mystic, it makes note that there's more. My Christianity doesn't stay inside the definitions most people attribute to Christians. My relationship with Jesus includes wonder, thinking outside the box, evaluating religious systems, and asking deep questions. It includes surrendering to his will for my life and desiring to be more like him than I want to be like me. Jesus touches every part of my life. My relationship with God is very spiritual. It is ever-evolving.

The classic Christian mystics[25] all experienced the Divine in a way that transcended time. They prioritized their relationship with God over all other things and wrote about the vulnerability and struggle and bliss of

---

24 *Lexico*, s.v. "mystic," accessed May 26, 2021, https://www.lexico.com/en/definition/mystic
25 Such as St. Teresa of Ávila, St. John of the Cross, Bernard of Clairvaux, and many others.

wrapping their human brain around the immense love they experienced between them and God. They embraced the paradox of unity and when they reached the end of their understanding, they accepted the mystery with faith. I don't believe this kind of relationship is a special gift set aside for a select few.

The Bible is clear that all are invited to the wedding, into unity with Jesus. It seems, however, only a remnant chose to open themselves and seek this depth of relationship. This continues to be the case and based on prophesy, that will not change. Intimacy and communion with God is a narrow path where only a select few choose to run. Running on that narrow path takes wholehearted pursuit, spiritual violence.

Jesus warned us that at the end of the age, "because lawlessness will be increased, the love of many will grow cold."[26] Whether it's a temptation to join in the lawlessness, or despair around the world getting so dark that God must be absent, as we approach the Bible's prophecies being fulfilled, it will be easier to fall away from God than to cling to love.

Christianity is not risking extinction.
God will not let it fade away.

There is and always has been a remnant who loved God enough to seek the narrow way, the path of intimacy with Jesus.
There is always at least one who stands in the gap and cries out for a fresh breath of his Spirit to breathe on the dead bones and make them live again.[27]
There will always be those who embody the spirit of Esther, knowing they were born for such a time as this.[28]
If you cling to Jesus, you will not be fooled by the doctrines of the culture and the false religions.

If you seek him, your love will not grow cold.

---

26 Matthew 24:12
27 Ezekiel 3:7
28 Esther 4:14

When we reach the end of ourselves, the end of our power and control, the end of all our seemingly brilliant ideas, all we can do is turn to the God who knows and sees all. We must align ourselves to his way and his vision for our lives, our country, and our world. God never changes. He is the same yesterday, today, and forever. The same God who sent plagues on Egypt and resurrected Lazarus can do signs and wonders today, through us, if we believe. He does refresh, realign, and heal the hearts, minds, and souls of those who cry out to him for help.

Like I said before, if we don't intentionally pursue God, we will get off course and start pursuing something else. If we don't love and trust God, we will look around at the lawlessness and the wickedness of the world, or the tough situation in our life, and decide God isn't good, or isn't acting on our behalf. But remember Joseph. If we stay walking with the Lord, then in both good and bad, he is with us. He still moves and acts on behalf of those who love him.

Before I continue, let's back up a little.

I said God loves diversity. I'm certain he does not want a remnant of clones, identical to the core. I might be a Christian-mystic medley, but someone else could be a different hybrid of Christianity and follow him just as well, maybe better! Christian spirituality exists outside denominational lines. We're all under Christ.

The Bible says, "There is neither Jew nor Greek, there is neither slave nor free, there is no male and female, for you are all one in Christ Jesus."[29]

In 1 Corinthians, Paul uses the analogy of our bodies to describe the community of believers. He says the foot can't look at the hand and assume it's less needed because it has a different purpose. He says the eye has no right to say to the hand, "I have no need of you." All the different parts of the body that some might disregard are actually indispensable.

---

29 Galatians 3:28

I've made his message a little more obvious for our modern ears:
> For the church does not consist of one person or group but of many. If the Pentecostal should say, "Because I am not a Baptist, I do not belong to the church body," that would not make it any less a part of the church. And if the Catholic should say, "Because I am not a Presbyterian, I do not belong to the church," that would not make it any less a part of the church body. If the whole church were Lutherans, where would be the Quakers? If the whole body were Orthodox, where would be the Progressives? But as it is, God arranged every person and group in the church, each one of them, as he chose. If all were the same, where would the diversity be? As it is, there are many denominations, yet one church. The Conservative Christian cannot say to the Liberal, "I have no need of you," nor again the Desert Mystic to the Fundamentalist, "I have no need of you." On the contrary, the parts of the church that seem to be weaker in their faith or opposite of you are indispensable, and on those sides of the church that we think less honorable we actually give more attention because without them on one "side," our "side" would not exist. Just like on our physical bodies, the parts we consider unpresentable are to be treated with greater care, mindful not to treat them with impropriety or indecency, which our more presentable parts do not require. God has composed the church, giving greater honor to the part that lacked it so that there may be no division in the church, but that everyone may have the same care for one another. If one person is oppressed for their perspective, all suffer for the lack of knowledge; if one ordinary person's view is glorified, all should rejoice together.[30]

God loves us all.
He loves and enjoys our diversity.
Diversity does not imply any lack of unity.
There is a difference between diversity and division.
God hates division. He delights in diversity.

---

[30] 1 Corinthians 12:14-26, adapted by the author.

There is so much division in our world. There are hundreds of religions and denominations, and all of them have pieces of the truth. But many hold onto their piece of truth tighter then they hold onto each other.

From the very beginning, the church struggled to stay united. There were arguments about circumcision, what food to eat, discerning the Spirit, and more. They had a lot of laws in their Jewish upbringing that had to be looked at through Christ's teachings and re-evaluated with the new revelation that Jesus' sacrifice paid for all sin.[31] These debates threatened to divide the people. There has been a war against unity since the very beginning and Satan still wants to divide us. The church is God's family, and the Enemy hates families. He hopes that he can convince us that love and unity is contingent on agreement, so when we disagree, we will stop loving and stop being unified. But the thing that unites this spiritual family isn't agreement. It's Jesus.

We look at each other and say, "Do you fit?" and God looks around and says, "You all fit." We are all his children, gathered from every tribe and every tongue and every nation. We are one big, diverse family. People who love Jesus are scattered all over the earth.[32]

Now, there are a couple of important things to note when we talk about unity:

First, being one in Jesus doesn't mean your individuality is erased. It means the perception of inequality is erased. Your gifts and talents are a unique combination made by God, and manifested in you. You are the one and only you in the world. To say you're the same as everyone else, would be to minimize and dishonor you. You were made for a purpose, and when you don't engage it, we all miss out. You have a unique place at the family's dinner table, and when you're not present at dinner, you are missed. Only you can bring your unique and special self to the table. You see things

---

[31] Jesus being the one sacrificial lamb for all people in all times, instead of offering rams and lambs and other at the temple daily, weekly, and seasonally.
[32] It goes without saying that there are plenty of people who claim to be Christian but do not love Jesus. Some of them are just wandering in the desert and will be back to their senses soon. Others don't know Jesus and don't plan to.

others cannot. You are good at things others are not. The community is not the same without you. Your diversity is needed. It is imperative.

Second, separation is not the same as division. Separation is good. Separation organizes. The hand cannot be the foot. The finger cannot be the arm. In Genesis, God separates night and day. He names things and calls them into their purpose and identity. He separates water in air and water on land. He clarifies similarities and differences. He puts stars in the sky, and gives them direction to "serve as signs to mark sacred times, and days and years."[33] God separates and organizes all of creation, including us, with purpose and intention.

Every tribe and tongue and nation is special and dear to the Lord. We are not meant to merge into look-alikes. We are meant to be a diverse family, standing united, with all our gifts and unique drum beats praising the Lord, side by side. We are each called to be different parts of the body. It's good that not everyone thinks or acts the same. We need people in different offices with different tasks. But all those offices and denominations must work together to glorify God and bring his kingdom down to earth.

The Lord's heart is that we would be near him and walk in unity with his family. When we say those who love the Lord are our "brothers and sisters" in Christ, it's not to be taken lightly. The Lord is a Father who wants all of his diverse family over for dinner at one big table. He wants everyone under the same roof and getting along, just like our earthly parents hope for on the holidays.

Families are not without problems. I don't know a single family who doesn't have the token addict, the weird rich uncle, or the run-away. But for the most part, everyone still gets together during the holidays. If you show up expecting to find people who are perfect, then you must be having dinner in heaven. You know how messed up you and your family is; Jesus' extended family isn't perfect either.

---

[33] Genesis 1:14

Spiritual Family || 153

We don't stop inviting our sister over for Christmas dinner when she's getting divorced. We don't stop inviting our son because he's smoking pot. We don't stop inviting our brother because he didn't make it onto the honor roll. Healthy families aim to create a welcoming environment with healthy boundaries where they can have structure and be seen and known and loved.

We need relationships.
We need community.
We need real hugs from real people.

In order to stay close to the Lord, we need to journey through life with people who will support us in our pursuit of Jesus. Things will bring you closer to the Lord, and things will take you away from him. Seemingly good things might actually be distractions, and seemingly bad things might actually draw you closer. We all need people who are passionately involved in the same things we are, whose individual flames help ours burn brighter. Passionate people ignite something in each other, and encourage each other to press on when things are difficult.

Our digital world is full of people with their noses in their phones who crave authentic connection more than ever. In order to get deep, meaningful, flesh and blood connections, we need to live in community. A spiritual community of diverse Christians is an invaluable, sustainable community of friends that sharpen[34] each other. Just as bad company corrupts good character,[35] a good community brings out the best in each other.

People who love one another can help each other stay intentional in their pursuit of God. They help each other stay positive and focus on Philippians 4:8, "Whatever is true, whatever is honorable, whatever is just, whatever is pure, whatever is lovely, whatever is commendable, if there is any excellence, if there is anything worthy of praise, think about these things." It is so easy to be sucked into despair by the state of the world, by the

---

34 Proverbs 27:17
35 1 Corinthians 15:33

lawlessness and wickedness that surrounds us. Community is a powerful asset in the fight to stay focused on what is lovely.

For me, staying focused on what is lovely has also required I follow Jesus so closely that I step on his heels. It's required a lot more than just being religious. It requires a desire for unity, a search for all things to be spiritual and have meaning. Marring the physical and spiritual world requires a lot of inner work and a lot of seeking. I ask God lots of questions about how he feels about things, from the food I eat, to where I spend my money, to who I surround myself with, to where I live and work. I ask him to be involved in everything because everything is spiritual. Everything I am, and everything I have, has been and will continue to be submitted to his leadership.

Some churches teach their congregants to go all in. The Bible teaches believers to go all in. But it seems like while Christians are told to do one thing, our culture demands another.

Individually, we are told to be like Jesus and his disciples but then, we are expected to be normal enough to get a job and save for retirement. If something we experience would rock the boat, we rub up against the culture of the church or the culture of the world, and we're shamed, ignored, criticized, or at best, simply misunderstood. If you are a missionary or a pastor, you might be placed on a pedestal, as if your calling is rare, but the truth is all followers of Jesus are called to proclaim the good news.

While we all have different callings, no one is greater and no one is lesser than all the others in the body. This is Jesus' family. Every role, every person is important. We all have a reserved seat at the dinner table. Corporately, there are other concerns when a church tries to go all in. For example, a church needs to be relevant enough to earn enough in tithes to pay for a multi-million dollar building. Getting busy Americans in and out as fast as possible for back-to-back services requires timed transitions and structure. Staying in business requires pleasing people and entertaining them. It might require flashing lights and great musicians, and sometimes,

Spiritual Family || 155

frankly, watering down the Word. Cultural expectations pressure the institution to stop the free flow of following the Spirit. These pressures often prevent churches from creating an atmosphere God's presence is invited to transform lives.

Jesus said "The wind blows where it wishes, and you hear its sound, but you do not know where it comes from or where it goes. So it is with everyone who is born of the Spirit."[36] God doesn't fit within our cultural expectations or submit to our fears of offending people. He is unchanging and yet, constantly moving. His Spirit goes where it wishes and he will fill any individual and institution where he is invited to be himself.

What if every believer actually did what Jesus said, including doing greater works than him?[37]
Then, we would be the church, everywhere we go.
We wouldn't just go to church on Sunday, we'd *be* the church every day.

Healing people would be normal, like it was in the book of Acts.
Seeing the Spirit move in power through us would be normal.
We'd walk by someone at the grocery store, and brush their arm, and they'd get healed and we'd introduce them to Jesus.

People seem to think pastors or priests or prophets are special or something. They place celebrity pastors on pedestals for having a special gift or connection to God instead of lifting up Jesus. Don't idolize them; they're human too. We're all supposed to live a life full of inspiration and Divine revelation and be filled with the Spirit. Jesus said, "The Helper, the Holy Spirit...will teach you all things."[38] The Holy Spirit is given to each and every believer who asks. You have just as much Holy Spirit in you as anyone else. You were chosen and your role is just as important.

We need midwives and teachers and doctors and plumbers and bankers and pilots and entrepreneurs and farmers and dentists and politicians and journalists and writers and artists and wedding planners and students to be

---
36 John 3:8
37 John 14:12
38 John 14:26

filled with the Spirit. Our world needs revival, first to the individual, and then to the system. Everyone has a part to play. Everyone is needed.

What if we actually united ourselves with the heart of the Lord and laid down our lives, so all our selfishness died? What if we built Jesus' name and his kingdom instead of our name and our kingdom?

***We could show the world what it actually means
to wholeheartedly follow Jesus.
It would redeem Christianity.
It would change the world.***

What if all this religion is just a masquerade?
What if it's still the same as it was in Jesus' time, a hypocritical system that he looks at with indignation?

What if cultural Christianity is actually a way that the enemy has been rationing spiritual water? Meaning, your shot glass-sized ration of water collected every Sunday morning in three songs, announcements, and a thirty-minute sermon, gives you just enough to make you feel like you've tasted God but leaves you thirsty and unsatisfied in life. The lie is that's all there is. The lie is that's all God will give you or all he has for you.

The truth is, you can have a direct connection to the fire hose of the overflowing water of the Holy Spirit. Going to church might give you an ounce or two. Jesus will place a well inside your heart, so you never go without.[39] Those two ways of life don't even compare.

Is the Spirit in these churches? Absolutely!

It's clear, God works within the religious system and the limits we've placed on ourselves and others. He is not containable. He is the Master of infusing goodness and life into all the messes we create. God is present anywhere people gather in his name.[40] But just imagine how good, how fruitful, how

---

39 John 4:14
40 Matthew 18:20

indescribable it would be, if we handed him the control, and said, "You drive our church, our home, our life."

At whatever measure you are doing this, trying to go all in and letting him drive your life, I commend you. God sees what you do in secret and will reward you for it.[41]

While being religious is defined as, "Faithful devotion to an acknowledged ultimate reality or deity," it is also defined as, "Devoted to religious beliefs or observances."[42] Being religious does not guarantee the devotion is pointed at Jesus. The Pharisees were quite religious, but their religious focus was in devotion to the law and tradition, not to wholehearted love for the Lord.

When the whole church unites under wholehearted love for Jesus, instead of religion, we will truly show the world what it means to love one another.[43]

My Mom and I love the movie, "A Walk in the Clouds."[44]

Keanu Reeves stars in a role where he poses as a pregnant woman's betrothed to prevent her from a shameful reunion with her family. When her Dad finds out the truth about his daughter, he grieves and drinks uncontrollably. In his drunken rage, he sets fire to the vineyard and destroys their livelihood. The story shows the father's journey from pride and arrogance to humility and remorse. It shows his definition of love being redefined, as he watches true love unfold in his daughter and a man she barely knows.

At the end, he turns to his daughter with nothing left to offer her except himself, and in the midst of all his family, he says,

---

[41] Matthew 6:6
[42] *Merriam-Webster.com Dictionary*, s.v. "religious," accessed May 26, 2021, https://www.merriam-webster.com/dictionary/religious.
[43] John 13:34-35
[44] *A Walk in the Clouds*. Directed by Alfonso Arau. Los Angeles, California: Twentieth Century Fox, 1995.

"I was afraid of losing you, all of you. I didn't know any other way to love. Can you teach me? Please...can you teach me?"[45]

I pray
we can unite the church
and learn how to love her
before
we accidentally burn it to the ground
for fear of losing it.

Lord, teach us to love.

I believe all we have to do is ask.

---

[45] Ibid., 1:31:11

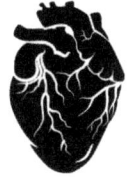

Invitation to Prayer

Lord, soften our hearts and teach us to love.
It's so common for us to fear loss, for us to think we have to hold things tight, for us to control however we can. Show us how to release these things to you and trust your way is better than our own.
We need unity.
Jesus, we want this generation to be the answer to your prayer in John 17, that we would be one as you and the Father are one. Sanctify us and make us a wholehearted, spirit-filled, united body of believers who show the world what it means to love you and others as we love ourselves.
Lead us not into temptation. Lead us away from pride and self-righteousness. Prevent us from judging others and measuring their worth according to cultural standards. God, give us discernment.
Bring me into a community where I am surrounded by people who love you and are committed to loving each other and walking through life together. I want to intentionally pursue you alongside others. I long for friends who will help me become my best self, who will keep me from stumbling and be honest with me, and provoke me in my knowledge of you.
And Lord, let these people be gentle and humble and not judgmental.
I know we are all imperfect humans, so Lord, above all,
I ask for people who are quick to repent and quick to forgive
and I ask that you would also make me one of those people.
I want to choose love over pride, but I will need your help to do it. I want to do your will and want the incense of my life to arise as a sweet-smelling offering to you. Show me my place, my role in the church body. Show me what my special place is in the family, and what you've called me to do, so I may live a fulfilling and fruitful life.
Amen.

The Invitation

One of the best parts of designing a wedding is creating the invitation. Sure, you can keep it simple and budget-friendly, some do. But when you go all out, for the wow factor, the anticipation of a once in a lifetime event is touched and felt by every guest the moment they receive it in the mail.

The invitation reveals the wedding colors, the theme, the attire required, and builds expectations through simple elegance and paper quality. It reveals the location and, my favorite part, might even include a map as if the guest will be searching for buried treasure. It tells guests things about the couple, the places they chose for guests to lodge, their favorite restaurants or hangouts. It shares a sneak peek into their private lives with the guests while they visit. These little touches make the invitation personal and one-of-a-kind.

Invitations are often further personalized to invite only the inner circle of friends and family to smaller, surrounding events. These special, limited, invitations ensure those who are closest to the couple get quality time and special attention. The carefully chosen words announce the uniting of two families, two lives. They request friends and family come to witness this monumental occasion, but also, which I consider to be even more sacred, to be invited into their love story.

Last but not least, the envelope includes an RSVP card, where the guest chooses to respond. They select, "Yes, I will adjust my life and travel to be part of this once in a lifetime event," or, "No, I decline for one of a myriad of reasons that are rarely shared."

Couples (often with the help of their mothers) spend much time cultivating the guest list and debating who to invite. From social obligations and business associates, to family and intimate friends, the guest count can become too large for the space they have reserved. Trimming the list and trusting that only those who are meant to be there will actually come, is one of the most stressful parts of wedding planning, and one by which nearly everyone is blindsided.

Long before the event, these stunning pieces of artfully printed and assembled cardstock are sealed and labeled behind colored envelopes and calligraphy and wedding-themed stamps and then mailed to those specifically chosen to attend.

And the RSVP cards begin to roll in....

It was not uncommon for me to relieve part of the stress around guest list creation by suggesting families create a B-list of guests. They might have people who they sincerely wanted to invite, but truly did not have enough room. As people declined, they could send out another invitation to someone who they hoped would fill that seat, and it would make the decline from their previous loved one much less bitter.

I had not found this to be an arduous process until my dear friend got married during COVID.

Instead of filling the role of the wedding planner, she asked me to be the maid of honor. I had never been a maid of honor. I asked her if she was sure. I thought there was someone more qualified for the job, maybe a friend who had known her longer, a cousin, anyone other than me. She disagreed. I resisted and pushed back and avoided saying, "Yes," as long as possible. I told her I would just do what I was good at and be the wedding planner, behind the scenes. She wanted me in that place of honor, even though I felt like I didn't deserve it.

I love my friend, so eventually, I caved. I wanted to love her more than I wanted to be comfortable. I remembered that it's not always about the amount of time you've known someone that makes them special or worthy of a certain place in your life. When things "click" into place, and you get a green light at every relational turn, you recognize it is special and rare. It's not always easy to find people who love well, and it is an honor to stand closest to the bride and her groom on their special day.

Everything in life will teach you about the Lord if you let it.

God is like my friend was in that situation. He almost haunts us when we try to go in a different direction. While we wrestle, he refuses to let go of what's best for us. He refuses to compromise in areas where we doubt our worthiness. He refuses to let us hide when he wants us standing in a place of honor by his side. It is important to put our love for him above our personal comfort. We must choose to stand by the Lord, even when it stretches us. He is worthy of the highest place and it is an honor to be near him.

While my friend planned her wedding, the typical guest list stress arose. Managing the budget and headcount was multiplied with COVID restrictions and the unexpected happened. The RSVPs started rolling in: no, no, no. I had told her it was normal for twenty percent to decline. In her experience, it was probably closer to seventy. Those myriad of reasons to say, "No," were multiplied by the complications and opinions of people during the pandemic.

I cannot explain to you the grief of a bride who feels like no one wants to come celebrate with her. I cannot express the heartbreak when the people you love most and cherish most are unable or unwilling to witness one of the most important days of your life. I cannot do justice to the pain of feeling like your love is rejected by others.

In her pain, I touched what the Father feels.
So many people decline his invitation.

> "And again Jesus spoke to them in parables, saying, 'The kingdom of heaven may be compared to a king who gave a wedding feast for his son, and sent his servants to call those who were invited to the wedding feast, but they would not come. Again he sent other servants, saying, "Tell those who are invited, 'See, I have prepared my dinner, my oxen and my fat calves have been slaughtered, and everything is ready. Come to the wedding feast.'" But they paid no attention and went off, one to his farm, another to his business, while the rest seized his servants, treated them shamefully, and killed them. The king was angry, and he sent his troops and destroyed those murderers and burned their city. Then he said to his servants, "The wedding feast is ready, but those invited were not worthy. Go therefore to the main roads and invite to the wedding feast as many as you find." And those servants went out into the roads and gathered all whom they found, both bad and good. So the wedding hall was filled with guests.'"[1]

Let's explore this and put ourselves in the Father's shoes.

How would you feel if you were throwing a wedding for your child, a once-in-a-lifetime event? You would be excited. You would have invested time and money into perfecting every detail.

How would you feel when none of your friends, neighbors, or business partners want to come? How would you feel when they're apathetic and indifferent? You would be heartbroken. You would be surprised and angry that they didn't care about you and that they cared more about going to work or providing for themselves than attending a party with free food and drinks.

---
1 Matthew 22:1-10

If, on the day of, you had food prepared to host hundreds of guests for many days and only a handful of people came, would you not tell everyone you know to come? Would you not tell everyone who was already there to call their friends so the food and music would not go to waste?

Many who are invited into the celebration of the kingdom ignore the call. They care more about their businesses and daily lives and the comforts or cares of this world. They care more about their selfish ambitions than celebrating with the Father. Others are angered by its implications, the way it imposes on them, or how it would require them to adjust their lives. They are offended and violently opposed to the dress code.

When you receive a wedding invitation, it specifies if there are any requirements for attire. Guests conform to the dress code as a sign of support and to partake in the celebration. If you intentionally rebelled and wore something different, it would be a direct affront to the host, choosing to voice your displeasure and refusal to celebrate. It would be like intentionally wearing a wedding dress to a wedding when you are not the bride. It would be incredibly rude and insulting. You would probably be kicked out.

Jesus ends the wedding parable with an encounter between the Father and a wedding guest. He says,
> "But when the king came in to look at the guests, he saw there a man who had no wedding garment. And he said to him, 'Friend, how did you get in here without a wedding garment?' And he was speechless. Then the king said to the attendants, 'Bind him hand and foot and cast him into the outer darkness. In that place there will be weeping and gnashing of teeth.' For many are called, but few are chosen."[2]

To attend the wedding, God requires that you dress appropriately. You can't get into the wedding by striving. You can't show up dressed in your own good deeds. You must be dressed in the blood of Christ. Paul says to "put on the Lord Jesus Christ."[3] He says, "in Christ Jesus you are all sons of God,

---
2 Matthew 22:11-14
3 Romans 13:14

through faith. For as many of you as were baptized into Christ have put on Christ."[4]

When you believe Jesus died for you and ask for him to cleanse and forgive your sins and ask for his Holy Spirit to fill you, you are covered by the blood of Jesus. To be Christian is to become a mini-me of Christ. It is to be part of the family, to become a son or daughter of God through faith in Jesus. That's the required dress code; to look like him.

When I was starting out in wedding planning, I would pay to set up a booth at wedding expos. This is where couples come to meet all different kinds of wedding professionals on a Saturday morning and try free cupcakes and enter to win prizes. I had the clever idea to spin off the traditional proposal of a groom to a bride and "propose" to the couples myself. I got the yummiest sugar cookies available in my area, shaped and iced like diamond rings,[5] and "proposed" to them as they walked by. "Would you let me be your wedding planner?" "Will you be my bride?" "Will you say yes?"

If the bride said yes, I would be engaged in their wedding planning process. (You see, the puns work so well!) It would be an instant transaction, to begin walking with her on her journey, but it would also be a process of preparing her for her wedding day, months or years from the start of our relationship. I was intimately involved in the process from that day forward. I helped with every major decision. I make connections for them. I tried to prevent them from making foolish decisions. I knew what they wanted and needed and ensured everything was executed as they desired on their wedding day.

My role as a wedding planner is a great analogy for how God works in our lives.

It's just like that. We say, "Yes," and he engages in the process. It's an instant transaction that saves us through faith in the holy blood of Jesus, and it begins a sanctification process that slowly overflows out of our hearts and into our lives. The internal transformation takes time to ooze into <u>every part of our</u> ethics, morals, actions, behaviors, thoughts, and so on.

4 Galations 3:26-27
5 I got Ring Pop® candies one year also. Fun fact.

Making Jesus the Lord of our life means letting him take part in every major decision, listening when he wants to prevent us from making unwise decisions, trusting his wise judgement and decisions, and asking him to provide everything we need. To live a Godly life, we must walk on that narrow path, where intimacy with God is our first priority.

The Bible says over and over that Jesus is coming back. It says he will return like a bridegroom. He has proposed and invited us into a relationship with him. For thousands of years, the message has been passed down from generation to generation: "Get ready; prepare yourself; he's coming back soon. You don't want to miss it, it could be any day now!"

It's true. It doesn't have to be true only in that Jesus will come to make the world new, descending in the sky, like the prophets and himself foretold. It's also true that none of us know how short or how long we have to live. Jesus could come for you or me, tomorrow.

For generations, this has been a message of fear, a message of "fire and brimstone." Preachers warn us the end of the world is near and we must get right with the Lord to avoid burning in hell. This misses the heart of the message. It might work to convince some, but God is not calling out to the world saying, "Do this, or else!" He is good. God is telling us, step-by-step, how to live, today. Every day, we run out of time to take part in his epic love story. Every day that we busy ourselves with the concerns of this world, we miss out on what we were created for; experiencing true life, abundance, freedom, and satisfying and wholehearted love with the Creator.

He is inviting us into his love story.
He is inviting us into a sacred covenant.
He's proposing. He's asking us to be his bride.
He's asking us to celebrate the wedding feast.

This glorious invitation has been mailed out[6] in waves for thousands of years. First to the Jewish people, and then, after Jesus came, to the whole world. Every tribe and tongue and nation was invited when the Holy Spirit

6 Not literally, of course.
Well, maybe, to anyone who received a Bible in the mail or in their email!

came at Pentecost. His Spirit fell on all people. No one is left out. All are invited to the wedding.

I love the story of Moses at the burning bush.[7] Moses didn't get an invitation in the mail, the Lord showed up in person to invite him into his plan. Moses was out shepherding a flock and saw a bush on fire, but the bush wasn't burning. The leaves were still flapping in the wind, totally unharmed. He was shocked and terrified and curious and approached to look closer at this mystery.

The Lord was watching for someone to turn aside from his work to gaze upon his beauty, and he called him by name, "Moses, Moses!"

Moses answered, "Here I am."[8]

While his mouth spoke, his heart was responding from a deeper place.

It said, "*I am fully present here. You have my undivided attention.*"

This wasn't a half-hearted reply, indifferent, or laced with fear of the Consuming Fire before him. No, when Moses met the Holy of Holies, he was captivated. He feared God, meaning he regarded him with awe and reverence. The last thing on Moses' mind was his sin and his past.

Moses had run away from his home and was hiding in the wilderness because his identity was confused and he was displaced. He was not accepted by his true family or his adopted family. He had run away from home and was enjoying a simple life in exile. But when he stood before the one who declares, "I AM WHO I AM," he said, "Here I am." He was not thinking about how he was hiding because he killed a man.

Most of us who are hiding or running from humans will also hide and run from God. Moses didn't.

---

7 Exodus 3
8 Exodus 3:4

God's presence was undeniable;
Moses had a radical encounter with the Creator of the Universe.

In Moses' story,
God meets a murderer with
self-doubt and worthiness issues,
who argues with God that he's not good enough,
doesn't know how to speak,
and literally asks God to send someone else,
and
God
doesn't
budge.

Moses had been *chosen*.
There was no going back.

God wouldn't give up on this man in hiding. God was patient and he took the time to convince Moses he had been chosen for a purpose. Moses argued, but for every doubt and argument Moses brought up, God had an answer. Never once did God tell him to go to practice his public speaking skills first, or repent for murder, or threaten to hit him with lightning for asking too many questions.

I'm a big fan of Moses. His story is so topical for our day. This is a man with a past who hesitantly steps forward into a crazy calling. He uproots his family and goes to challenge Pharaoh, the most powerful man in the world, who is also his kind-of ex-step-brother. Talk about family drama.

I doubt that is what Moses wanted to do with his life. He didn't dream about risking it all to end up wandering around in a desert following God. I think he would have been pretty happy living on the mountain with his wife and children into old age, but he wouldn't have been satisfied. The true joy that came to Moses when he saw God move in signs and wonders to set his people free and part the Red Sea could never compare to his lukewarm happiness in his previous way of life.

You can't measure
how much better life is
in partnership with the Lord.

Moses had the free will to wake up the next day and pretend his moment with God at the burning bush never happened. He could have ignored the invitation, buried it, and disobeyed. He could have run away like Jonah. He could have let his self-doubt stifle him. He could have convinced himself that he had spoiled meat for lunch and the bush was a fever dream. After all, the next day, the bush would have still been there, unburned. There would have been no evidence, no way to prove that his encounter with God was real.

All he had to rely on was faith.

Our journey doesn't always make sense. Especially when we have a big and scary dream. Your God-dream, the purpose and plan for your life, will probably scare you. You will probably feel like you're not good enough or you don't know enough, like you're not ready to do it. God loves to come and fill the holes. He wants to complete the picture where you are lacking.

You don't have to be perfect. You just have to be willing.

Moses was only kind-of willing at first. But like a mustard seed, his faith and willingness grew. He found God to be faithful and as God performed miracles, he longed to draw closer and closer to him. The invitation to walk with him is instant, but the transformation is a life-long process. Later in the story, years later, Moses says to God, "Please show me now your ways, that I may know you in order to find favor in your sight."[9] I love this part of the story, because God replies, "My presence will go with you, and I will give you rest."[10]

Moses comes to know, after years of experience, the only thing that matters is to be in-step with the Lord. He can do anything with the Lord and <u>nothing without him</u>. His one and only desire is to meet with God face to

9 Exodus 33:13
10 Exodus 33:14

face and dwell in his presence. The heart behind his question is, "Please tell me what I have to do so that we will always have an intimate relationship like this." God answers, "You have my favor already. I will go with you. You don't have to work for it. I will give you rest and comfort and peace."

That's all we need.
His presence to go with us.
That's heaven on earth.

One of the most common Bible verses referenced at weddings is what the widow Ruth says to her mother-in-law, Naomi, when given the choice to stay or return home to her old life and her old culture. She clings to Naomi and says, "Where you go I will go, and where you lodge I will lodge. Your people shall be my people, and your God my God."[11]

I pray this often.
"Lord, be not far from me.
I desire your presence.
Where you go, I will go.
Where you stay, I will stay.
Your people are my people.
You are my God."
As if they are wedding vows....

When Moses leads the Israelites out of Egypt, God meets them in the desert. He appears to them on Mount Sinai and proposes to the people with vows to betroth themselves to his presence. God says, "If you will indeed obey my voice and keep my covenant, you shall be my treasured possession among all peoples."[12] And all the people say, "We will."[13]

They enter into a covenant,
and then God leads them step-by-step,
day and night.

---
11 Ruth 1:16
12 Exodus 19:5
13 Exodus 19:8

God does not stop when they grumble. He does not stop when they build idols for themselves and bow down to man-made gold statues. He does not stop when instead of being grateful for their simple life, simple food, and ability to rest, they complain about how they used to be able to eat all the figs, grapes, and pomegranates they wanted when they were slaves in Egypt. Of course, he gets angry; he's passionate and has a personality and emotions. They wanted to go back to slavery so they could eat better! But he loves them. God sticks by their side, even when they complain he's not enough.

We are no better.

We work our butts off for rich food and glamorous experiences. We bow down to the pharaohs of this world and become slaves to our debt and demanding work schedule. We grumble and complain that God's covenant is too hard a thing to bear. Still, he's right beside us. He never leaves our side. He never breaks his side of the vows.

God's directions and promises are good. They are always for our benefit. He's a good father. Jesus reminds us, fathers do not give their sons stones when they ask for bread, or scorpions when they ask for eggs.[14] Jesus says if good fathers on Earth know how to give good gifts, then even more so, our heavenly Father gives good gifts, abundantly, to those who ask.[15]

Asking empowers us.

You are not helpless when your best friend is the Creator of the universe.

But so many people, deep down, don't believe that God is good. Many think they must work for God's favor. Many believe God is against them because of their past. There are lots of ways Christianity has become twisted, perverted, and simply misunderstood by the masses.

When we read our Bibles and seek the knowledge of God, not to get something, not to memorize it or take a theology class, but to actually get

---

[14] Matthew 7:9; Luke 11:11-12
[15] Matthew 7:11

to know his character, his personality, his desires...we fall in love with God, with Jesus, who came in the form of a man. That God-man, Jesus, is captivating. *He is so easy to love.*

If you get to know him, you will love him.
If you already love him, you know him.
And if you don't yet, all you have to do is ask.

Then crack open a Bible.
Read the love story.
Don't read the Bible for facts and information.
Read to seek the lover of your soul.
God is your true soulmate.
You were created to love him.

That's the unique purpose of your life: to love him the way only you can. Any spouse here on earth is the lover of your body, mind, and heart, (hopefully!) but he or she can't move your soul the way God does. There really is a God-shaped hole there that only God can fill, no matter how cliché that might sound.

Eugene Peterson writes that, "Christian Scriptures are the primary text for Christian Spirituality. Christian spirituality is, in its entirety, rooted in and shaped by the scriptural text."[16] We read the Bible to "assimilate it, [to] take it into our lives in such a way that it gets metabolized into acts of love."[17] He says, "Every word in the book is intended to do something in us, give us health and wholeness, vitality and holiness to our souls and our body."[18] Scripture, the Word of God, is what shapes and molds our souls.

The Bible, the Word of God, is the most powerful tool you can use to shape your life. It is more powerful than any self-help book, any sermon, any life experience. It points us to the things that really matter. It sets our priorities straight. To be shaped, primarily, by something other than the Word of God

---

16 Eugene H. Peterson, "Eat This Book" (Grand Rapids, Michigan: William B. Eerdmans Publishing Company), 15.
17 Ibid., 18
18 Ibid., 22

is damaging to the soul. "An interest in souls divorced from an interest in Scripture leaves us without a text that shapes these souls."[19]

But why does it shape us? How?

John calls Jesus "the Word." He says, "In the beginning was the Word, and the Word was with God, and the Word was God. He was in the beginning with God. All things were made through him, and without him was not anything made that was made."[20] This is why people say the Word is living and breathing and active.

It's alive; it's Jesus.

Scripture, the Word, is the revelation of Jesus. You cannot be made new without him. All things are made through him and developed by him.

Paul calls Jesus the chief cornerstone.[21] A cornerstone is the one you shape all other stones to be like, so all the stones in the building are the same, and they fit together seamlessly. The Word shaves down our rough patches and sharp edges to make us like the cornerstone, Jesus.

The Word *transforms* us.
Combine your faith in the blood with the Word,
and you will have a fancy wedding garment.
These things make us, his bride, beautiful from the inside out.

This kind of surrender, to be shaped and molded, to have our hearts circumcised, our minds renewed, our souls restored, is what Jesus is looking for in his bride. This surrender comes when we believe that God is active and working in all things, in the in-between space, connecting everything to everything else, everyone to everyone else. It's when we genuinely long for a real, intimate relationship. We surrender when we are vulnerable with God. It's where we find comfort and peace and settle into the unknown. It's when we truly enjoy the curious mystery of this ineffable

---
19 Ibid., 17
20 John 1:1-3
21 Ephesians 2:20

God who loves us unconditionally. It's when we are happy to enjoy the view and let God navigate. It's when we accept that we are loved and accepted, and invited to be in communion with the Divine; every moment, of every second, of every day, just as we are.

God is in the transformation business.

The only constant in life is change. That's why the only thing we must be consistent about, is loving God, and loving others as we love ourselves. Personal growth and intimacy with God are the only things that really matter in our life. We are here for relationships. And there are three kinds: with yourself, with others, and with God.

It's easy to look at our failures in these areas instead of our progress. We consider our rocky life and see how unlike the cornerstone it looks. We see how far we have yet to go, but God remembers and cherishes every time you were willing to be filed down and shaped bit by bit.

In one of Paul's letters, he advises that we be like him, and not even judge ourselves[22] because only God knows our heart. Our hearts can deceive us. Even we ourselves do not know our own intentions sometimes. When we think we are pure, we may be in fact biased. When we think we are failing, we may in fact, be succeeding.

Only the Lord knows and sees all.

Spiritual transformation moves at God's speed. Sometimes, that's a pause. You can't count and track what God is really doing in someone else's life. Don't get me wrong, you can see the fruit of their transformation over time. But at first, only the Lord sees and knows how the seeds are growing under the surface. When we think something has died is exactly when the seeds of something new are beginning to sprout.

I've seen plenty of people stop doing traditional things and get closer to God than ever before. Whether we like to wander in the desert or God

---

22 1 Corinthians 4:3

purposely takes people the long way around to find him, it seems like our adventurous journey with God is a scavenger hunt. Only he knows what we're looking for and where to find it. Everyone's journey, process, and transformation is one of a kind.

Just like every love story is one of a kind.

Your story will not be the same as my story. How he speaks to you is not how he speaks to me. Some are called to show their love for him in prayer and fasting. Some are called to show their love for him in building soup kitchens or ministries or businesses. Some are called to love him by raising adopted children. And some are called to all of these things, for a season, and other things in different seasons. We all have different ways of loving him, and all are needed in this family.

God says, "I desire steadfast love and not sacrifice."[23] He wants us to know him and love him. He wants our actions to overflow out of a love for him and others, not out of an obligation to do certain things a certain way. Just as a groom would not want a bride to say yes to his proposal because she felt pressured, but because she truly loved him, God also wants a wholehearted, "Yes."

He wants to build a love story with you.
He wants to build rapport over time.
He wants to walk through every detail of life with you.

He wants a conversation with a friend about the heartbreak they're going through while they struggle to forgive. He wants a conversation with a friend about the excitement he's feeling because he met his soulmate. He wants a conversation with a son who cares for his elderly mother, and to teach him how to honor and respect and love her well in this season of life. He wants to use every opportunity to transform you.

When we partner with God in the process,
he walks with us through our messy lives.

---

23 Hosea 6:6

Only a God who loves us unconditionally would want to do that.
No other god claims to do that.
All the other gods want people to serve them.
Jesus wants to serve *us*.

On the last night Jesus spent with his disciples, before he was crucified, he washed their feet. He showed them, if he, the Lord, served and loved them with humility, they should serve and love each other with humility. He says, "I have given you an example, that you also should do just as I have done to you. Truly, truly, I say to you, a servant is not greater than his master, nor is a messenger greater than the one who sent him. If you know these things, blessed are you if you do them."[24]

He desires that we love him, and that we love one another.
There is a blessing in this kind of love.
It's the unity of family.

When my friend was walking down the aisle, everyone was moved to tears. The groom was crying, the guests were crying, and I was praying to prevent myself from crying. I was asking God to give her peace and strength. I was asking for their marriage to stand the tests of time. I was asking God for help with all the things I could not control.

He replied to me, "This is your family."

Standing in the room, witnessing this wedding, was a group of people that had grown to be close friends in only a short time. I looked around. There we all were, witnessing the first of us to get married. I had always hoped and longed to find a group of people that would choose to be friends for life. Other people found their crew in college and stayed in touch. I wanted a group that did life together. I wanted to be in a community where my kids would become friends with my friend's kids. We had all talked about a future like that, and only God knows if it will happen. But that day, I was watching it unfold before my eyes.

---

24 John 13:15-17

This group had witnessed my heart get broken and helped me heal. We had prayed with each other when our family members faced hardship. We had contended and fought side-by-side in those many hours in the prayer room during our internship. We considered each other battle buddies. Many accusations and fears had come our way and threatened to tear apart our relationships, but we chose to stay together. We had conflicts and worked through them. We were not perfect, but God was right, we had become a family. A family not based on our bloodlines, but on the blood of Jesus.

My Ruth prayer had been answered.
His people had become my people.
His family was my family.

I had been invited to a wedding. I had resisted the part I was supposed to play at first, just like Moses. But when I said yes, God used it to transform me. He uses everything to transform us.

Now, I officially extend his invitation to you.

God wants you to return to love. He will use every season of your life to transform you and fill your heart with gold, especially your desert seasons. He will use the rollercoasters of life to build your faith in his faithfulness. He says you are worthy and wanted. He deeply delights in you. He wants to be your closest and most intimate friend. He will lead you step-by-step, just listen and obey the best you know how. He will take care of everything else. He has a special place for you at the dinner table. He wants you in his family.

Even more so,
he's inviting you to be his beloved,
his bride.

Will you
"love the Lord your God
with all your heart
and with all your soul
and with all your mind?"
Will you "love your neighbor as yourself?"

Everything depends on these two things.[25]

Jesus is asking.
I'm inviting.
All you have to do is say *yes*.

---

[25] Matthew 22:37-40

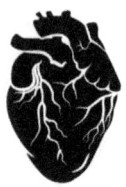

Invitation to RSVP

In your own words, have a conversation with the Lord and tell him, "Yes, I will adjust my life to love you with all my heart, mind, soul, and strength and take part of this once in a lifetime event."

If you are speechless,
or want to take some inspiration from Ruth & I:
"Lord, be not far from me.
I desire your presence.
Where you go, I will go.
Where you stay, I will stay.
Your people are my people.
You are my God."

No matter where you are or how many times you've vowed to him before,
the invitation to go deeper, abides.
The invitation to know him more, always stands before you.
Remember, he is like the ocean. He is ineffable.
You will never run out of things to learn,
and he will never tire of your questions.

*"Behold, I stand at the door and knock.
If anyone hears my voice and opens the door,
I will come in to him and eat with him, and he with me."
Revelation 3:20*

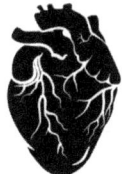

Continue on the Journey

I would love to hear from you.
Seriously, I'm giving you my phone number....

Sign up for emails, shop merch, & connect with Alena at
alenavandyke.com
505-252-7689

If you are walking through a difficult season or transition,
want to heal your heart, and return to wholehearted love,
I'd love to work with you.

alenavandyke.com | miniphanies.com | prayinthedesert.com
Listen | Miniphanies™ Podcast
Insta | @alena.vandyke
@miniphanies @prayinthedesert

About the Author

Alena Van Dyke is a spiritual mentor, author, teacher, speaker, podcast hostess, and friend to wounded hearts. She is an 8 with a very strong 9 wing and an ENFJ.

As a modern Christian mystic, Alena believes **everything is spiritual** and encourages you to **expand your God-box.** Through writing, teaching, and enjoying deep and meaningful conversations over coffee, Alena joins others on their journey to seek the Lord with **all** their heart, mind, soul, and strength. Alena is an encouraging and welcoming companion for those walking through difficult seasons and into a wholehearted life with Jesus.

In a time when the heart of the Lord is misrepresented, and the name of Christ misused, Alena is a clarifying voice for modern Christian living. She speaks the truth without hype or hypocrisy. She is unafraid to address real issues in religion and church. With a gentle and loving approach, she deconstructs toxic religion and extends an invitation for believers to reconstruct a healthy, deep, and meaningful relationship with a loving God, their neighbor, and themselves.

Alena has dedicated her life to a true and deep understanding of what it means to follow Jesus. She earned a BA in Religious Studies at the University of New Mexico, and an MA in Spiritual Formation from George Fox Evangelical Seminary. In 2019, she left her award-winning career as a wedding planner to dedicate herself full-time to ministry and served in the Nightwatch at the International House of Prayer in Kansas City. After delving as far left and as far right as you can get in Christianity, she aims to teach and live life in the middle, a biblical balance between legalism and cheap grace. Today, Alena is a prophetic voice crying out in the desert for souls to seek the Lord with wholehearted pursuit.

In the Miniphanies™ podcast, Alena shares ancient truths in relatable ways, inspired by everyday experiences. These simple ah-ha moments, *mini-epiphanies*, inspire you to live with intention, choose spirituality over religion, and wholeheartedly embrace the Golden Rule: loving God and loving others as we love ourselves.

In her first book, *Return to Love*, Alena shares her journey and wisdom gained in spiritual valleys, mountaintops, and deserts. It is a practical guide and invitation for those seeking a deeper relationship with God. She is currently writing her second book, a candid discussion of something Christians won't talk about: divorce.

She is also the founder of *Pray in the Desert*, where believers gather together to pray, heal, and worship Jesus in the beautiful state of New Mexico.

Alena lives in Albuquerque, New Mexico where she is determined to obey the Lord, seek his face, and create a place for others to meet him in the desert, find healing, and worship under the starry sky.

Alena is available to travel and teach, lead retreats, or connect for deep and meaningful conversations over coffee.

A little Love for my BFFs

To the Lord, first and foremost....
Thank you for staying with me night after night, at all hours of the night, to write this book. Thank you for carrying me through the transformation that was required to write these words from the confident place of personal experience, and not letting me lose myself or you in the process. Thank you for pursuing me, even when I ran away like Jonah or argued like Moses or laughed like Sarai. Thank you for being the Spirit of Inspiration, my Faithful Father, the lover of my soul. Oh, how I love you.

To my Mother, for all your support, physically and spiritually. I think praying with me every night is what led to finishing the first draft of this book. Little did we know the power of a mother and daughter coming together in prayer. I love you, and I'm so thankful for all you've done to help me flourish in this life. Thank you for witnessing my transformation, reminding me how good God is, and being my life-jacket when I felt like I was drowning. I am so blessed to be your daughter.

To my Grandma, the librarian, who passed on to me her love for books and taught me to enjoy the little things, like coffee with mint meltaways at the end of a long day. I am so thankful for you and your love.

To my team of cheerleaders:
Renee, Steffanie, Jac, Jarah, and Paul & Stephanie.
If it were not for you, I would have tapped out. Thank you for not only believing in me, but for praying for me and holding onto God's promises when I was too weak to hold them. Thank you for holding up a spiritual mirror to remind me who I am. Thank you for being my spiritual family. You are truly God's gift to me. I love you all.

Steffanie, you are the one who has always believed in me and supported me, from the *very* beginning, even recommending me for seminary. Thank you for investing in me, always loving me, and trusting me as a friend and godmother. I am honored to call you a sister in spirit.

Renee, thank you for the many spiritual conversations over coffee that have helped shape who I am. Thank you for bringing out the best in me, believing in me, never judging me, always cheering me on, and holding me accountable to go all-in. I am so blessed by you and your friendship. My life is richer with you in it. You're stuck with me forever.

To Dan, thank you for designing the heart in a day. You are amazing and wonderful and arrived at just the right time to help both my book and I return to love....

*If this book inspired you
or gave you some mini-epiphanies,
I hope you'll share it with a friend.*

*Until next time,
from the bottom of my soul,
thank you for listening.*

www.ingramcontent.com/pod-product-compliance
Lightning Source LLC
Chambersburg PA
CBHW050331010526
44119CB00004B/128